LEARNING TO HUNT

LEARNING TO HUNT

MARK S CLOER

XULON PRESS

Xulon Press
2301 Lucien Way #415
Maitland, FL 32751
407.339.4217
www.xulonpress.com

Paperback ISBN-13: 978-1-66286-062-1
Ebook ISBN-13: 978-1-66286-063-8

This book is dedicated to the memory of
'Brother Bob'.

My brother-in-law Bob Vogt. He was the person who opened the door into this incredible world and started me on my journey. From the bottom of my heart Bob, I thank you for lighting the fire within. Through these humble works, it is my sincere hope that fire will remain lit long after I am gone as well. Bob lived his life on his own terms and left this world in exactly the same way.

Know that you're missed Bob, but your passion lives on.

Preface

The stories in the book are all true. They are a culmination of events that occurred as a middle-aged male set out to teach himself the right of passage that is hunting. As it can be with many men, stubborn pride and a "DIY attitude" were the cause of most of the mishaps along the journey. Many of those events were quite humorous although these comical mistakes also packed a valuable lesson. I'd like to share these events with as many people as possible. I wish to raise the awareness of, and the love for the outdoor life associated mainly with, though not exclusively for, hunters.

It is my intent to use those mistakes to entertain hunters' who have been in the field since their grandpappy taught them how to hunt.

I also wish to reach those who in one way or another had to learn themselves the hard way. Perhaps they can relate to the stories the most.

I would like to increase the overall understanding about outdoorsmen. In any sport there are different levels of players. Say in football, you have the Jerry Rice's of the game. The guys who can do it all, do it extremely well but do it humbly. You know... the guys you want your kids to emulate. ROLE MODELS. Then there are the other guys; loudmouthed poor sports whom you don't want your kids to even know exist. But they do! Hunting is no different. There are indeed the guys who just hunt so that they can kill an animal. There just are! The vast majority of us fall somewhere up the ladder. It is my intention to take that majority further up the ladder of awareness and increase (if possible) their love for our sport.

It is also my goal to connect those who hunt with those who don't. Though our perspectives are different, they may not be as far apart as one might think. As it is in politics, there are extremes on both sides. There are those who would kill for what they might call fun, and there are those who think that we should just eat paper plates instead of putting food on them... Again, most of us end up somewhere in the middle. Common ground is attainable. I wish wholeheartedly to reach out to those people (like my father) who just don't want to kill an animal. We understand! We really do! We want you to be able to experience the primal force of the outdoors. You don't have to kill to feel it; you simply must be aware of its existence. Most of the love and passion that we have for our way of life comes from simply being out in nature; seeing, feeling and understanding what goes on in the deep woods. Come and enjoy, be our guests. Don't allow our difference of opinion to stand in the way of all of us communing together with nature. We indeed understand your way of thinking. Please try to understand ours'.

The group that I would truly like to connect with the most is our future hunters. No matter what age they are. Each of the stories told have an antidote. You will find them at the end of each story. They are written in italics and highlighted in bold print. If you wanted to have the condensed version with just the lessons, then just skip through the book reading only the italics. That would be my version of Cliff's Notes. The advice you receive would be the same as you might get from your grandfather. The long version gives not only that lesson; it gives an entertaining example of why it's important. By exposing myself and my MANY MISTAKES it is my sincerest hope that I can shed the light of experience upon all who wish to learn more about the tradition of hunting.

Who says learning can't be fun?

Hunting is not brutal savagery. It pits the predator in a fair and balanced conflict with its prey just as it is in nature everywhere. Where the cheetah can outrun the wildebeest, it can only do so for a short distance. If the wildebeest population were not kept in check by its predators, then it would soon overpopulate the tundra and consume the food resources for all the other animals, who would then starve. The delicate cycle which nature has set in place has worked since the dawn of creation. Only human arrogance would suggest that it is wrong or that it does not work.

No, hunting is not savagery, in fact it places humans right where God intended for us to be... at or near the top of the food chain.

To hunt for part of my existence, take down an animal and then properly prepare its meat and transfer it into a feast with my own hands has turned into one of the most fulfilling experiences of my life. While I do not necessarily consider myself an authority on hunting...I do consider myself an authority on

"Learning To Hunt."

This is my story...

TABLE OF CONTENTS

PRELUDE

Having the day before shown Michael proper shot placement I allowed him to try out the different weapons which were available to him. Quietly, I assessed his shooting ability and deemed him ready for his first hunt. I placed him in the barn, a place where he could be comfortable dry and warm. It was also a place where the deer had been seen in large numbers and had not been harassed. The shot, if he was fortunate enough to get one would not be too long and the field was clear. Lastly it was right beside the cabin so if he wished to end his morning hunt before I did, he could simply walk over to the cabin unload his gun and go inside for breakfast. That was extremely important to me since I was not going to be able to retrieve him from his stand and walk him back. I was looking for a very nice ten pointer that I had seen on my trail cameras on the back side of the property. I was planning on still-hunting to the western most section of the property. For those of you who don't know, still hunting is the art of stalking through the woods in search of your prey. That would be no easy feat since the elongated drought had made the ground cover in the hardwoods like walking on dry cornflakes. I knew I was in for the whole first half of the day at best.

My trek began at the creek which cut the 180-acre property in half. It ran from north to south. On the opposite bank was an overflow flat area which under normal conditions was a swamp. That was not the case this year. As such, it was not the great spot that it usually was. Having learned over the years that a good hunter must change and adapt with the conditions. I had opted to work my way up the hill behind the swamp. My destination was the top of the knoll where a thick cedar grove invited the monarch to make his home. Under a west-southwest cross wind, I began to move west through the crusty swamp at the first light. My movement pattern was a constant state of extreme slow motion. I was attempting to make myself appear like a part of the surrounding trees while making forward progress. Every few feet I would once again scan the area in front of me and to both sides with my binoculars for any sign of a bedded deer...ears flinching, antlers twisting around, the flick of a white tail, anything which would give away the animal's hiding place. Movement and noise are two primary give aways. Still-hunting in the crunchy leaves was placing me at a distinct disadvantage. The deer I was seeking was lying still and making no noise at all while I was moving forward and producing noise. The ground noise I was producing was an intentional perpetual crunch. The never-ending sound produced no breaks with which any animal in the area could compare the silence to. In my mind I was trying to mimic the sound of a turtle slowly crawling across the forest floor. Hardly something that would put a bedded deer on high alert. The two advantages that I had over the buck was that he was expected to be asleep after a planter's moon the night before. And, by using the crosswind, I was negating the use of his nose, his primary defense. I stealthily continued on.

By around ten o'clock I had advanced about halfway up the hillside and was still some five hundred yards from the cedars where I presumed the buck to be bedded down. The good news was that I had not been blown out by any other deer in the area. The bad news was that I was getting tired and thus the potential for getting sloppy was very real. I found a downed oak tree maybe fifty feet away and worked my way towards it for a much-needed rest. Even at rest I was hunting. I found a comfortable place to lean up against the tree and doubled my efforts with the binoculars while giving my body a break from the constant workout that is still-hunting. That's when the familiar sound of my 30.06 erupted throughout the woods. Michael had taken his first shot at a whitetail deer. I was beyond stoked, remembering the time I had been fortunate enough to take my first animal.

This turn of events set a new clock in motion. I was slowly nearing my destination. I knew that I had done nothing to this point to give away my position or my intent. I was close but not there yet. Now my excitement for my brother-in-law was starting to twist my arm in another direction. I knew that Duff, my hunting buddy would have his back, but I wanted to be there when he retrieved his first deer. At the same time, I had gruelingly inched my way towards the hunt I had been planning for weeks. I decided to continue, thinking by the time I got back to where they were; I would have missed the event anyway. Rested and rejuvenated from Michael's hopeful success I began to move towards the tree line and my own deer. About halfway between the tree where I had taken a break and the suspected bedding area, was an old logging road. It ran parallel to the tree line. When I reached that spot, I stopped again because of the vantage point the somewhat clear road provided. I had begun to see deer movement in front of me heading towards the tree line. Not the buck I was hunting but a good sign all the same unless one of them busted me. From the road I could see north and south clearly, and I was also in shooting range of the woods that were my original goal.

I had lost the advantage of a covering wind due to an unexpected wind shift. Now the winds were out of the south southeast. It was time for a change in my game plan. Knowing the chances of continuing into the bedding area without getting scented were not good, I turned my attention towards the old roadbed. I got just inside of the brush on the western side of the road and started into the new wind using the road as my guide. Keeping my focus on the bedding area to the west I moved down the road. There were occasional glimpses of does moving in the cedars. I caught movement roughly halfway up the hillside to my right.

Glassing confirmed that there was a buck bedding beside a downed tree. I could make out antlers through the limbs of the tree but could not see them well enough to tell what he was. All I could do was wait or move forward. I tried waiting. After a half an hour I decided to try moving. I began towards the sleeping buck stopping to glass every few steps until finally I confirmed what I was stalking. He was a very tall six pointer. He was a beautiful animal for sure and given a few years he would be king of the woods but not this year. Over the next thirty minutes I covered the sixty yards south without alarming the buck. He was now directly west of me and forty yards up the embankment. Still, he hadn't detected my presence. I continued to move on past him as quietly as I could. The road eventually bent off to the left and more into the wind. I was moving towards the end of my still hunt and I knew it. When I reached the point where the wind was now working against me my scent found its way to the big fella and sent him on high alert. He jumped up, snorted and took off like a scalded dog.

I sat down on the cold ground and gave my heart a chance to slow down while I reflected on what had just happened. I had still-hunted three quarters of the way up a mountain in crunchy leaves seeing animals all along the way. I had picked off a sleeping buck and then still hunted ninety yards by him without alerting him of my intrusion. At one point being no more than forty yards away. I was only given away by my scent and only at a point beyond my control. My still hunt was over for that day. Happily, I picked up my bow began the trek back to the cabin to see what Michael had done... having never taken a shot on one of the greatest hunting adventures of my life!

First Impressions

My first impression of hunting came when I was nine while on a trip with my dad. Seeing another father and son having breakfast together decked out in cool looking cloths that looked like trees. I asked my father what that was all about, he answered "they've been hunting". Now my father was about the greatest man, father and friend I've ever known so I was puzzled as to why we didn't go hunting together. We fished together, he coached my baseball team, and he was even involved with the Y Indian Guides with me. That was another organization where you got to dress up. When I put the question to him, he simply stated "my dad never taught me cause he couldn't shoot an animal, neither can I and that's why I haven't taught you." He seemed so adamant that it was wrong that I never brought it up to him again. Yet I always wanted to know more about this secret society of sportsmen. It would be many years before I got the opportunity to finally experience one of the few things my dad had deprived me of as a child. It wasn't his fault! He didn't know the passion that many of us have for the woods. Neither did he understand the primal instinct that we still have to fend for ourselves and our loved ones.

Light The Fire

The first year I married my lovely wife Dianne, I took her to Japan for Christmas... Japan Missouri! Well, it may not sound quite as exciting as it's more famous namesake, but for me that trip was my first hunting experience. Well, almost. My new brother-in-law Bob had at the time; an incredibly beautiful cattle farm called KiKi Run on which he raised breeding stock. The second evening that we were there, Bob invited me to go hunting with him in the morning! Holy Crap! I was finally going to find out what it was all about! I hardly slept at all. Bob woke me well before the crack of dawn. We went down to his basement, and he rummaged up some camo for me and an extra pair of rubber boots, explaining to me that they would help to keep my scent off the ground. Visions of the adventure to come flashed in my head as I waited to see what type of weapon he had chosen to loan me. "Let's go" he said without handing me my weapon. "What am I gonna shoot" I asked? "Nothing, you're gonna watch and learn" he countered. So off we went on my new adventure with me not even armed enough for a mouse let alone "bear".

Bob set me up in a tree about 20 yards from his bow stand where I could see all the action. Now just because I grew up in the city didn't mean that I didn't know anything at all about the woods, after all I was an Indian Guide. I was fully aware that woodsy owl "gave a hoot" ... what I was not aware of was that 20 feet up in a tree a real owl right in back of you at five AM can scare ten years growth out of you. I almost fell from my perch! I never knew if Bob had quietly witnessed the entertainment. He never mentioned it and neither did I. I suspect that if he had, he may have come dangerously close to falling from his own perch...laughing! He didn't take a shot that morning, but I did see my first deer in the wild. He asked me later if I saw the two deer. "I saw one" I stated. Apparently there was another directly under me for ten minutes that I failed to notice. One out of two ain't bad. When asked if I wanted to go with him again in the morning I immediately answered yes, even though I didn't think I'd get a weapon that time either. I was right.

He didn't shoot his bow that morning either, but I received my first three hunting lessons... *first you don't get to see deer every time you go hunting. Second, you must have a hunting license for whatever state you are hunting in. The fees from licensing go to make sure that the animals you are hunting are preserved for future hunters as well as for themselves. And third and most important, **you don't have to shoot an animal to have a great hunt**. It's all about being in the woods and enjoying nature. It was much later that I discovered a fourth lesson that my quiet brother-in-law taught me in those two days without my realizing it. **You never put an untrained novice in a stand with a weapon and allow them to shoot at an animal.** In every aspect, it is the wrong thing to do. It's dangerous! It's unfair to the animals because at best case the hunter would probably wound them. Quite honestly, it was not necessary for me to be armed to become hooked for life. Bob taught me the single greatest lesson of my hunting career... **Hunt for the hunt, not the kill. The pleasure is truly in "being there".** From* the bottom of my heart, THANKS Bob, you lit the fire!

OK so now the fire is lit. I'm now off on a new venture. I was going to become the hunter

I was born to be. Trouble was, while the spirit was willing the flesh was weak. Maybe I should paraphrase that a little. While the mind was willing, the body had absolutely no clue how to go about it. As it is with many men, I don't do instruction manuals. Christmas can go either one of two ways... cussing & throwing a fit of rage or the present that says "some assembly required" has a picture on the box like it should. I can figure things out on my own just fine. First get a license. Second buy a weapon. Third find a place to practice shooting. And finally climb up a tree at an ungodly hour so the deer will come out on cue and allow you to shoot it. Really how hard could it possibly be?

First Blood

**"We are a culmination of our trau-
matic experiences!"**

My adventure with my brother-in-law happened at the end of hunting season so I
would have time to prepare myself for the next
season. One spring day I was looking around
an antique store. I like the old handmade tools
sections. They always seem to put these in for
husbands whose wives drag them along while
they're looking at furniture. Any way I stumbled across a bow. Now strike one, two and
maybe strike three should have been finding
your hunting weapon in an antique store. All
the same I found myself at the check- out
counter with the bow in my hand. Twenty dollars later, my hunting career had begun.

Now remember, I was an Indian Guide
so bow shooting was a skill I had already
learned. Truth be told, I was pretty good at it

as a kid. That was with a recurve. This fancy "new" gizmo was what they call a compound bow. It was camo, and had knobs, wheels and widgets on both ends. I knew I could figure it out without asking for help. All I needed was some arrows. When I went to the local sporting goods store to purchase the arrows, the guy at the counter wanted to know what my draw length was. "Oh about average" says I. Jeff (who would later become a good friend) just kind of smirked a little and said "about 31 inches I'd guess." What kind of a bow are you shooting" he asked me next?" "It's a compound" I proudly answered. (I had no idea what the name brand on it was.) With those horrifyingly technical questions behind me, I became the proud owner of thirty dollars' worth of fine high-tech aluminum Easton arrows. They were about as big around as my thumb and weighed about a half pound a piece. And they were camo, so they matched my bow perfectly. Turns out they matched it in more ways than one. I found out years later that my 'hooky bow' as it would become known was an old Pearson. It had a draw weight of about 100 pounds. I think it was originally owned by one of Homers heroes in the odyssey. Like Odysseus, I took great pride in the fact that no one else at hunt camp could draw my bow.

So now I was set! **I had all the gear I would ever need**. All I had to do now was practice becoming a great shot like William Tell, Robin Hood or "Hiram Walker" (you know that Indian feller) who shot his arrow "in the air" ... the "where it lands I know not where" part I had down pat in no time at all.

I went out to my warehouse with no one else around and started my lessons. I knocked my first arrow, wrapped my bare fingers around the string pulled it back looked down the arrow shaft at my paper plate target and let "loose". Bink! I think that's the sound I was rewarded with as my first five-dollar arrow crumpled on the side of one of the refrigeration cases that was kind of, sort of near the target I was aiming for. "OK, that was a little left". I tried again. Much better; no bink... in fact no anything at all. While not as far left as the case that my first arrow "found" my second five-dollar arrow was still left enough to miss the target and disappear into the hay field never to be found again. I quickly came to the realization that hunting could get expensive. Not one to give up easily... er... ah ever, I loaded another of my V-2 rockets. I aimed still further to the right and

"WALLY" as they say in France. (Well southern France anyway.) I hit the paper plate followed by another "Bink" as my third five-dollar arrow crumpled up on the case that my paper plate target was duck taped to. OK, OK so I needed to make some improvements on my practice range but man, on just my third attempt, I hit the target! I found something "less solid" to attach my target to and continued with my lessons. By the end of that first day I had bloody fingers, a bruised left forearm from string slap, quite a few solid hits on my improved target. Last but not least I had no more arrows. Upon my return to Nichols Store to buy more arrows, I told Shannon I wanted six Easton 31-inch arrows. Wow I was even beginning to sound like a hunter! And I was only eighty dollars in. What a deal!

I continued to improve (since I had little elsewhere to go) over the next few weeks until I was probably the most accomplished bare fingered no sited compound bow archer in the area. Alright I didn't know it at the time, but I was the **ONLY** bare fingered no sited compound bow archer in the area, but I *was* good.

As hunting season began to approach, I went back down to Nichols Store to buy my first license. By now I was starting to become sort of an irregular regular. The fellow who sold me the license was a likable person. We struck up a conversation and I began to confide in him about my newly found passion for bow hunting. "What kind of sights are you using" he asked me? "I'm just looking down the arrow shaft" I told him. "And you're hitting something" he questioned? Dead center every time I truthfully and proudly answered him. He seemed truly impressed. "What type of release are you using"? Something about the guy seemed to say that I could just be honest with him and not get embarrassed. "I don't know what a release is" I confessed. He gave me the same kind smirk that Jeff had given me a few weeks back and said, "come on with me". Darren, the owner of Nichols Store quietly took me aside and explained that a modern compound bow (which of course I didn't have) needed to be fired with a release. He showed me the different types he had in stock and politely helped me choose an inexpensive one that worked as good as the pricy ones. He tried to sell me on some sites, but I refused to budge. By now I was hitting everything I aimed at without them.

I took my new release back to the warehouse. I put it on my arm the same way Darren had showed me at his store. I knocked an arrow and pulled back on the release and drew first blood! The release was not set for such a high draw weight and when the tension reached its' peak it just let go. The result was a self-induced right hook to my nose. I stood back up, dusted myself off and I took the "defective" release back to Darren. He told me that it was the way they were designed and helped me to adjust the tension on the trigger. Once again, he seemed impressed. This time that my draw weight was 100 pounds. I was too dumb to know the difference. To this date whenever I draw my bow back, I put my finger against the back of the trigger to keep it from firing before I want it to.

Never be afraid to ask if you don't know. It's true that people want to laugh, but there is a greater truth in life... **people would rather feel important, about being the person with the answer, than laugh at you.**

Dream Season

The name dream season implies the perfect hunting season. One where everything goes the way it is supposed to and culminates in the perfect animal ending up in your sites, and ultimately on your dinner table. Maybe I should retitle this chapter! No, on second thought, this is the correct title. It's just got a different connotation from the first impression I mentioned. It was merely the season that I had dreamed of for so long. For certain everything did not go right! I have a small piece of land on which my warehouse is located. Not that I knew it at the time, but it happens to have a perfect funnel on the back side of the property. It's a tree line that's approximately sixty yards wide and it runs for nearly a mile. It divides most of the properties within that mile +- area. Of course, I wasn't planning on hunting the funnel for that wonderful reason at all. The season before my brother-in-law Bob had hunted in the woods.

He had hunted from a tree stand. And he had hunted with a bow. That was as much as I knew about the sport at the time, so it was the natural choice.

Right as the season got started, I filled up my truck with lumber, drove it down to the wood line unloaded it and proceeded to build a fort in a cedar tree. I hammered, sawed, hauled and cussed for two days. By the time I was finished, there had to have been a gallon of my sweat on the ground. Not to mention the usual number of bent nails, blood and urine. I was finished all right... for the first part of my season at least! I'll bet there wasn't a deer in that whole mile long section of woods! None the less that very next morning I climbed up my new wooden steps to my tree fort to do battle with the monarch of the forest. Now imagine trying to work your way up a tree in the dark using nailed on two by fours for a ladder while holding onto a four-foot compound bow and a hand full of arrows. Ted Nugent would have been envious of the decibel level I must have produced. After I pondered on it for a few minutes I decided that a rope would be helpful in hauling up my gear the next time. Not to mention safer. In fact, I could invent just such a thing and make some money at it. (That would be the first of many inventions I have come up with for hunting only to find out that I was not the first hunter to face such a dilemma and come up with a solution.) There I sat for several hours sweating and swatting mosquitoes, peeing over the side of the stand perhaps even humming a little tune to pass the time. Lesson one learned from brother Bob turned out to be true. You don't see deer every time you go in the woods. In fact, for most of that first season, it turned out to be more of the norm. Gradually by watching hunting shows I began to learn about things like the wind direction, scent control, being still, being quiet... you know hunting stuff. Still no deer. I needed help. Finally, I called Bob. His answer was classic Bob, short and to the point. "Why don't you try an evening hunt?" I'm thinking all (both) times you hunted it was in the morning so that's when I've hunted but I said "sounds like a good idea to me" thanked him for his time and started planning for an evening hunt. It was considerably easier. I was already at my favorite (only) hunting spot when I was at work. I just cleaned up a bit, climbed my favorite (only) stand and hunted till dark. The third evening I tried it I struck pay dirt...well almost. A young buck came in and started to browse. My heart was pounding like a jack hammer! I stood up, got into my normal shooting position, drew back my bow...wait a minute, where had the deer gone? He left before I was ready! How rude! It would be a very long time before I was successfully able to draw a bead on a deer with a bow, much less take the *shot*.

There's a great advantage to being a do-it-yourself kind of person. We are the take charge people of the earth. **But don't confuse stubbornness with self-reliance... Again, if you don't know, ASK.**

At this time my sweet wife Dianne was working as a domestic paralegal for an attorney named Mike. Mike wasn't your typical lawyer. He had put himself through law school setting tile. He could be as direct as a father with a school child. Many times, Dianne would overhear him asking a client "what were you thinking?" Or "are you crazy?" There have been times in my life when I wish I'd had an attorney talk to me with such good common sense. Mike was also an avid hunter. In fact, my wife called him a fanatic. She said "he loses his mind during hunting season. It's all he thinks about"! (Much later, she would wonder why I couldn't be a more reasonable hunter like Mike was.) Mike gave me one of his typical "what are you thinking" answers." Hunting is too new for you to be using a bow. You're too close to the deer. You need more experience. Get a gun!" Straight forward and to the point great advice, that's Mike. We became great friends.

THE SHOT HEARD
ROUND THE WORLD

I took Mike's advice and brought my old shotgun out of retirement. I had an old Thurston Motor Lines van that I used for extra storage down in the field about 75 yards away from the stand I'd been hunting out of. I cut a window out of the side of it and "Wally"...(aka viola for those of you who bother to speak French!) Instant ground blind. Now I had two stands. From that ground blind, I took my first shot at a whit tailed deer. This led me to two realizations about shooting. First buck shot doesn't do a whole lot of damage at that range... *so know your guns limitations*. Second... well imagine being in a 45-foot tractor trailer van and then shooting a shotgun! It was like a canon going off! I felt like "rain man" when the fire alarm sounded! Never in my life have I again heard anything quite that loud...*so the* *second lesson about shooting, **wear hearing protection**.*

I spent the rest of that first season hunting regularly with little to show for it but little to discourage me from continuing to try. I continued to seek advice from Mike as well as Bob but if there aren't any deer in front of you then you can't very well harvest one. Other than the one shot out of the trailer; I never got the opportunity to redeem myself. So much for "Dream Season."

It's Not What You Know
It's Who You Ask

Even with my first full season behind me there was no way that I could claim veteran status. Even so I had come in my own enough to admit that I needed both information and help from those who knew more than I did. Now the answers to my very discreet questions that I been asking (in one way or another) were slowly beginning to sink in. I eventually became so comfortable with the staff at Nichols' and with Darren that I finally fessed up to what they had known all along... I didn't know Jack squat about hunting! Not only was it not nearly as painful as one might think, I actually began to get the questions answered in ways that made sense to me. Before when everyone continuously talked about scent control...I just thought I was kind of stinky. When someone would question my weapon choice...I naturally thought they were just trying to sell something. Now that I admitted what everyone else knew, they could explain their comments to me in ways that weren't offensive to my male ego. Since my ego was no longer in the way (well at least not as much as before) I could just ask a question instead of tap dancing around it. Often, I would get two or three opinions and would have the luxury of deciding which one sounded right for me. I could finally begin to be taught how to hunt and what to hunt with.

NEVER be afraid to ask or to admit that you don't know something. It's the only way you'll ever learn!

Now that I was primed to listen and learn, the first thing I needed to change was my gear. Camo from K- Mart, rubber boots from Tractor Supply, homemade deer stands... I may as well have been Elmer Fudd stalking through the woods with a pop gun "hunting wabbits." With this new-found attitude, Darren was able to talk me into purchasing my first hunting rifle. It was (and still is) a Winchester Mountaineer 30.6 with a synthetic stock. He had me mount a nice Simmons scope onto it bore sited it for me and explained how to site it in. However, he failed to mention that it was (and still is) a mighty powerful rifle to be housed in such a light stock. Like the "Hooky Bow" there aren't too many of my hunting buddies who are able to (or willing to) shoot it, at least not more than once. I worked with my .6 for most of that spring.

BWANA

Spring led to summer and since I live on the lake much of our summer activities revolved around water. You know sailing, skiing, swimming, sunning and of course playing off the dock with Aspen, my Siberian Husky. Now a lot of my neighbors also have dogs and participate in water sports with them so it's kind of a neighborhood weekend thing. One day I get a business call from a guy who is looking for someone to get his walk-in cooler hooked up. Nothing out of the ordinary about that, it's what I did at the time. What was different was that this guy wanted to use his cooler for processing his own deer, not everyone else's. I said sure I could help him. In the course of sales small talk, we got around to where he lived... in a lake side community called River Hills Plantation. "What a coincidence, that's where I live" I countered. We continued to talk. It turns out he liked a lot of the same things that I did fishing, hunting, boating, playing with his dogs in the lake... he had a beautiful big-headed black lab named Hank and cute little yellow lab pup named Kaki... "wait a minute, you're the guy across the harbor from me. I'm the guy with the husky." Well, we met down by the dock to seal the deal over something else we both liked to do, drink a cold beer. Turns out that Vernon had a beautiful farm in Chester County called Balenacre. It was his very own hunting haven. He took me out there, to see the cooler that I was to do the refrigeration work on. What a place! It had a rustic cabin with all the amenities, a well-stocked pond, acres of cleared fields and plenty of hard wood. It was time for some more horse trading! "I'll put a new condensing unit and evaporator coil in your cooler and get it running and you let me join your hunt club." We would both end up with way more out of the deal than that. For starters Vernon, whom I would later dub as Bwana (the great white hunter from Tarzan) knew everything about hunting that I didn't. And... he was willing to teach me. For my part, I was to provide him with years of entertainment as I tried to learn what he was teaching me. Vernon introduced me to the rest of the guys in the club. They were all very likable people. Each member was very different from the next. The first person I met was Jey. He was a big country boy. An ex-Citadel football linesman. He was also one of those guys who grew up hunting. I quickly learned that any time that Bwana wasn't around I could count on Jey to help me. Whatever job I was working on or answering questions I had about hunting, farming or the outdoors in general. He and I became great friends. Then there was Joe. He was the mystery man in the group. We hit it off fine. Joe was just kind of a quiet to his self-kind of guy. Like Vernon, Joe is very successful and well respected in his field. He reminded me of my brother-in-law Bob. He can dress up and go anywhere and fit in... but he seems the happiest on his old tractor plowing a field. My kind of guy. And last there was Earnest. He was a customer of Vernon's. A good hunter as well and a heck of a golfer. They were a very diverse group indeed. Each one of the guys took me under their wings a little bit and showed me the ropes. That was a great thing for me because I had a lot of questions.

For starters "why was the place named Balenacre?" Vernon, was once told by an interviewer conducting an aptitude test that, "he had an uncanny capacity for storing (useless facts)." He had gone down to the county deeds office to research his purchase. In the post-civil war tax records, he found the boast that this farm yielded a bale (of cotton) an acre. BALENACRE. Useless facts indeed, that's cool stuff! That's Vernon. Another "have to know" question was why do you call your hunting property a "farm"? "That's a question better answered when you're up on a tractor". It turns out that it takes a lot of knowledge to be a successful hunter. Farming is one aspect of that knowledge. Knowing how to plant crops, which crops to plant, where to plant them even the shape of the plot; all of this is important to a healthy huntable herd. Well, it didn't take any time at all for me to realize that growing up in a city does not exclude a guy from being a farmer at heart. I loved it. I couldn't get enough of it! Truth be told, I'll bet I spent as much time working at Balenacre as I did hunting on it. Never have I had another hobby or activity that I was involved in that I would play hooky from work just so I could go there and work my can off! Now at this point in my life my wife said I was going through my mid-life crisis. No, I didn't go buy an old muscle car and soup it up. I didn't get a motorcycle, or start chasing hot chicks. Instead, I would climb up under an old tractor to fix a leaky gas tank, I went in on a four wheeler with Bwana, and I was far more interested in hot does than chicks. I even started listening to country music! Rock n roller that I've always been...that one made her stand up and take notice! On any given weekend you could find me going up and down the fields on old blue with my Kenney Chesney hat on singing "I'm looking sexy on my tractor"...Ok maybe I had the words a little backwards, but you get the picture. So, with all the fields planted and sprouting their new crops for the fall, Vernon began my tutelage into the world of an "outdoorsman". He began with how to scout a property so that when the season finally did come in, you knew where to intercept the animals. What a novel idea, outthink the deer! More importantly, WHY one area would be used by the deer, while another would not. It was all really confusing. Why did it matter whether there were acorns up in the trees where the deer couldn't even reach them? Saddles went on the back of a horse. Funnels were used to change the oil in your truck. Rubs seemed like they should be called scrapes since the buck scraped the bark off the tree, and scrapes should be called rubs since the grass and leaves were rubbed out of the way. As mid-September came about, the new future Davie Crockett pulled out the big bow and began to hunt. I actually began to see deer! Regularly! Hunting and seeing deer are very different from shooting at one. I might see a deer within range, but it wasn't a shooter. Or, I would see a shooter, but it wasn't within range. I remembered how difficult it was to draw a bow on a deer. When you're close enough to shoot one, it's easy for them to catch you moving. During all the dilemmas and setbacks, I began to notice a change in myself. I've always been extremely competitive. Three weeks into the season with no kills in sight and I'm having a ball. No tantrums, no I'm ready to quit, no desire to nudge the odds in my favor by cheating. Even when I didn't get a shot, seeing deer, was enough to satisfy me. REALLY? Who was this guy? This was way more than a mid-life crisis. I was born again.

Always strive to be successful at whatever you try **but don't allow winning to replace the joy of being out there trying...no matter what it is you're doing.**

First Kill

Muzzle loader season found me hunting with the old Pearson since at the time I didn't own a black powder riffle. One morning, Bwana shot a doe with his flintlock. He found me and showed me how to blood trail the animal. When we finally found her in the apple orchard, she was still alive. Vernon hadn't reloaded, and of course" you can't use a pistol for **any reason** during black powder season". Vernon is a true stickler for the letter of the law. He quietly and gently almost lovingly leaned over the scared animal, patted her neck till she calmed a bit and then surgically used his knife to put her down. To this day, I've never seen anything quite like that! Who were these" hunters"? They could kill a deer, but still love them enough to feel compassion for a suffering animal. Even if they were the one who had caused the suffering. Never, in all my hunting years since, have I received such a powerful lesson.

"To be a great hunter, one must both love and respect the very animals that one hunts". Even as I wrote this segment, some twenty years later, I teared up. So natural at it was he, that I wonder if my buddy even remembered the incident. I of course will never forget it. **I thank you brother, for teaching me to hunt. But thank you even more for teaching me...about hunting**

Gun Season

I was so, into my newfound self that one fall afternoon I showed up at the farm to work on the disk. When I turned down the road, I found Vernon and Earnest already there. I was really confused; it was no big deal to have Bwana show up at his own farm to work... but Earnest? It turns out it was opening day of gun season and I didn't even know it. They thought I had shown up to hunt and I was there to work. Oh yeah, I was so busy being a farmer that I forgot that I was gonna be a hunter! Hunting season was here at last, and I had no gun, no camo nothing. Well, I borrowed some of Jey's ill-fitting cloths and Vernon's shot gun went down onto the ridge above oak hollow. Looking like a homeless person I climbed up a tree.

The oak tree I climbed into was about 60 feet up a steep escarpment with another thirty to go to reach the top. The deer were coming from down in the creek bed bottom and moving up the hill to feed in the oaks. It was the perfect set up. The stand area had been previously scouted by my new buddy Jey. He had done all his ground homework and transferred his knowledge into the place where I was now waiting in ambush. The only flaw in an otherwise perfect lay out was that Jey was no great fan of heights. I was no higher than twelve feet off the ground. Still, I was in the perfect place. I was forty minutes into the sit when a pair of deer began working their way up the hill right towards my stand. My heart was beating like a piston. The smaller doe was being followed by a nice sized buck. She led him right underneath the tree that I was in. I was immobilized! We were practically eye to eye at less than ten yards apart and yet they didn't know that I was there. The two of them grazed under me for the longest few minutes of my life. I was too scared to move. Finally, the doe lost interest in the acorns and began to wonder away from me taking the buck in tow with her. With his attention now focused away from me and enough distance between us for me to raise the shot gun, I took aim and shot at my first deer since the trailer incident. He jumped about three feet in the air, stumbled and then took off in a wide circle back down the hill in the direction he had come from. Now I had been watching hunting videos and knew that I needed to wait the proper amount of time before I lit out after him. So, I dutifully waited...almost a full two minutes (or as close to that as I could) and then half scampered and half fell out of the tree. I had remembered something about visually marking the spot where the animal had been standing when the shot was taken. "The woods"! That's right, he was standing in the woods. I was almost sure of it. Frantically I searched for the spot where my deer had been when I shot him. It was to no avail; I was too hyped up to remember exactly where he had been standing. What I could remember, in fact still see in my head was the last place that I saw him as he ran away. OK that could work! I went to that spot and started searching for blood around there like Vernon had showed me. That was about the time he and Earnest showed up to see what I'd shot. Now that's hunting part-ners! There was still daylight left and they both sacrificed the rest of their opening day of gun season to come celebrate my first kill with me. All three of us began the search for a blood trail but for the next twenty minutes we came up short. Bwana had me get back in my stand while Earnest played the part of the deer. That was truly working. I could mentally play back their actions and was able to direct Earnest back to the spot of the shot. Just about the time that I'm expecting to hear some good news I heard Earnest say, "did he look like this?" He stepped aside a bit and revealed an oak tree with a very brightly skinned up trunk. I had missed the deer and shot a tree. "Tree Killer" became my very first hunting nick name. That's also hunting partners. If your hunting buddies are good enough to stop their hunt early to come celebrate with you on your first kill...then they're good enough friends for you to allow them to pick on you. We all went back to the cabin laughing. But there were still some more lessons to be learned. Vernon set up a water jug on the fence post and had me shoot at it. Oh God I thought, what's gonna happen if I miss? Well, I didn't miss. I nailed the water jug. Spray went everywhere. "That's what a slug will do when it hits something" he said. "There should be no question next time as to whether or not you made a hit if you are using a slug gun."

Always know the weapon that you are going to use when you go hunting. There can be and often are some nuances about it which can only be learned by firing it. It's the safe thing to do for you, and the fair thing to do for the animals.

Blood trailing an animal is not voodoo. It is an acquired talent. It requires nothing extraordinary on the part of the tracker other than an awareness of your surroundings. It requires alertness to the visible signs. And also an ability to remember the events which lead up to the shot and those after it. For those of us who have "less than adequate" memory skills, the answer is flagging tape. When you see blood or broken twigs... flag it with something. After a while, step back and look at the overall picture. The direction of the flags will tell you which way the animal was heading. When all else fails, reenact the event. Get back in your stand, and have another hunter play the part of the deer.

Taking It All In

I was having the time of my life hunting. It was turning into everything I had hoped it would be. While I myself had yet to kill a deer, my buddies were quite successful. Every one of their victories not only turned into one of mine, but they usually ended up with a lesson. By paying attention and asking questions, each event was a chance to learn more. I became a sponge. I remember the first time I saw a deer skinned like it was yesterday. Not only because it was something that I would need to know, but it also doubled as a great lesson about when **NOT** to humble someone. In this case that person would have been me. I helped Vernon take a doe that he had shot to the skinning rack. I then helped him hang her and then cranked up the winch. Vernon gave me a knowing glance that was unperceivable to the others in the group. The look said, "I know you don't know how to do this yet, but I'm not gonna say so in front of everyone else." In his years of being a scoutmaster, he had perfected showing a new skill without belittling the recipient of the lesson. He simply took a half a step aside. He looked over his shoulder to make sure I was paying attention and proceeded to quietly show me how it was done. At each critical point in the process, he would quickly look back over his shoulder as if to note that this was an important step. I watched and learned. A lot more than just dressing out a deer. All while the others in the group were clueless as to what was happening...

You don't have to make someone else feel small in order to look like a giant. My buddy's sense was dead on for this occasion. I quietly took in both lessons never to forget either again.

"Just Shoot Something"

Eventually in every new hunter's learning curve there comes a point in time when the only thing left to do is "pull the trigger." That was the consensus towards me by the other members of our club. Now up to this time, I had been following all the club rules on shots taken. Those rules of engagement are or should be pretty standard in any hunt club. Bucks were to be eight points or better and their racks, outside of their ears. Does could only be taken on scheduled doe days unless you had purchased doe tags. These simple rules will help to insure a healthy QDMA heard. Well, as a new hunter, I had been following those rules to the letter. The trouble was, I was seeing plenty of four and six pointers but no eights. I was seeing plenty of does, but never on doe days. Everyone was worried that eventually I would get frustrated and quit. I knew that wasn't going to happen. I was having a great time just being out there and finally seeing deer. It was thrilling to me whenever one of the other guys would take an animal and allow me to be in on the trailing and gathering. Their success was my success. This is the way it should be in a group of hunters. None the less, I wanted my success to be their success as well. So did they!

In preparation for a successful hunt, I washed all my camo and prepared all my gear. That of course included cleaning my gun. Thoroughly! The next day I got up extra early and drove out to Balenacre. I got to the cabin just shortly after everyone else had left. I stood and stared at the map of the property, which also served as our sign in board. I finally choose my spot, tagged in, and off I went. The stand I chose was called the Low Boy. Why? Because it was low! It sat not more than ten feet off the ground in a clear-cut triangle. There were hardwoods at the top of the triangle, ugly, thick pines for bedding on another side and a creek bed down in the bottom. See, I was learning. I knew where I was going and why! It didn't matter that the stand was so low to the ground, the morning sun was at my back. This made it hard for any deer coming towards me to catch me in the stand. The hunt was going along uneventfully until about nine. Just then a nice looking six pointer came out of the bedding area. He stepped about five yards into the open and then did something that I had never seen a deer do, or since, for that matter. He stood up on his hind legs and surveyed the field! "That was so cool" I thought. He then started straight towards me, stopping along the way to do it again, twice more. "This is a smart deer" I thought to myself. At about fifty yards away, he stopped and turned broadside to me. I thought "let's have some fun". I very slowly pulled my riffle up and took aim at him. "Boom, your dead" I whispered to myself. The deer turned around the other way and offered me his other side as if to say, "have at it buddy". I raised my gun again, found him in my sights and thought "got you again"! "This is good practice" I thought. Then it dawned on me that everyone had absolved me of the eight or better rule in favor of me finally shooting a deer. "Why not" says I. "Let's do it". I raised my gun yet a third time only this time, I wasn't playing around. I was going to shoot him. He was walking at a slow pace by this time. He was heading right towards a medium sized oak tree. "Perfect" I said to myself. "When he comes out the other side, I'm gonna nail him!" He slowly disappeared behind the tree, but he wasn't coming out the other side! I was beyond confused. This was like a bad episode of Popeye and Pals, or the circus clowns. They go in one side but don't come out the other! And I was going to shoot! REALLY SHOOT. I must have watched that tree for ten minutes. "This can't be happening" I thought. He never did reappear. About thirty minutes later I hear Vernon's I'm coming in signal. I'm still sitting there...stunned. "What'd you kill" (our familiar greeting after each hunt) he said. I couldn't even answer him at first. I simply climbed down out of the stand. "How was the hunt" he re-greeted me. "Different" I countered. "How so" says he. I told him the tale, beginning with the buck standing on his hind legs. "Well, I'll be" he said. "That's not the whole story"... I proceeded to tell him about the disappearing deer. He didn't laugh, he didn't pause, he didn't even call me a liar. He just pondered the event for a minute, turned on his heels and said, "follow me". Of course, I did. We went straight over to the tree that I had been talking about. Mind you I had never told him which one it was. He knew exactly what had happened. When we got there, he began to laugh. "It's not funny" I protested. "It is too" he said. When I got up to the tree in question, I could immediately see it all... Why he knew exactly which tree I was talking about. Why he didn't think I was making the whole thing up. And why he was now laughing so hard, that I thought for sure he was going to pee himself. There, directly in back of the other side of the tree was a draw. The "disappearing deer" had gone down the hill on the other side of the tree and proceeded to follow the draw up to the safety of the tree line another forty feet away. Just then it hit me as funny too! We probably scared every deer in the county away with all our laughter. That could only have happened to you" he crowed. "I know, I know" I was able to get out between breaths. We walked back to camp laughing the whole way. "Well", I said, "we won't be hunting in that area this afternoon. I may as well hit the range and take some target practice". "Good idea" said Vernon, "I'll join you." We walked down to the shooting bench. Vernon walked across the dam to the pond and set up a target on the other side. It was measured out for 100 yards. I loaded my gun when Vernon returned. I sat down at the bench, put the gun on the pillow and let one rip. "Nice shot" said Vernon. "Yea, I just cleaned my gun last night" I bragged. "Try again" he said. Boom, the 0.6 sent another round speeding to its target. Now Bwana knew that I had really put some time in on this bench and it had paid off. Boom, another round totally dead center, right through the mark of the first two rounds ... "Wait a minute" said Vernon, "I know you've been practicing. You've gotten really good, but not that good. Take a shot at the upper left target." Boom... no hole. I chambered my last round and fired at the same target with the same results. "You missed the whole damned board" said Vernon! "Mark, when you cleaned your gun last night, did you take the scope off?" "Well of course I did" I said indignantly, "I cleaned **EVERYTHING**!" "You dummy, you never take your scope off! We'll have to re sight it. Let me see your gun" he said. I handed him the rifle. He sat down at the bench and looked through the scope. When he set it down, I noticed a puzzled look on his face. He placed the gun in the pillow and moved back away from it to get a better visual. He began to shake. Slowly at first then harder and harder, I realized he was laughing. If possible, he was laughing even harder than we did about the "disappearing deer." He couldn't seem to stop long enough to let me in on the joke. Tears had formed under his glasses and still he couldn't talk. As I realized that he was laughing at me, my ears began to get hot. "Not a good idea Vern," I thought. It was kinda like when Chubaka was losing at chess to R2D2. Hans warned that "Wokie's were sometimes known to pull the winners arms out of socket." C3PO said "I've got a new strategy R2, let the Wokie win!" He finally got it under control enough to show me what was sooo funny. Not only had I messed up all the practice I had put in with my gun by taking my scope off, it seemed that when I put it back on, I missed one of the housing mounts for the scope. The barrel of the riffle was going one way, and the scope was going off to the left, kind of like an off kilter "X". "It's a good thing that that deer disappeared, cause if you had pulled the trigger, he would have fallen over... laughing... ah ha ha ha over and over he kept laughing until the Wokie saw the humor in the situation and decided to join in. When the laughter finally subsided, Vernon set about to undo what I had undone. He did a fine job of remounting the scope and then bore sighting the riffle. He then sat down at the bench, placed the riffle in the pillow and squeezed off a round. The viscous 0.6 practically stood him up. It was the Wokie's turn to laugh at Bwana. Rubbing his shoulder, he said "you messed it up, you sight it in! I'll spot." Vernon has never shot that gun again!

Know the topography of the land you're hunting. *It's just as important as knowing where the bedding areas or feeding areas are.*

Don't try to clean a weapon that you're unfamiliar with. ***If you don't know something about the process, ask someone who does.***

If you're teasing a friend, ***know when it's enough, and when to back off.*** *If a friend is teasing you, take it in stride and enjoy the humor of it all. Fun is fun.* ***Don't be a hothead!***

FINALLY

The following weekend I ended up out at the cabin with Earnest. Saturday afternoon Earnest went to the Heart attack stand. So named because the previous year he had a heart attack while trying to drag out a deer that he had shot from it. I went to a stand at the very front of the property called the scaffold. It was a box stand that had been set up on a scaffold. Not very creative names, I know but they told a story. In fact, most everything at Balenacre told a story. That was part of the magic of the place...it had history. Anyway, I hunted the scaffold that evening. Right at dusk, I heard movement behind the stand. I turned myself around and saw a young doe at the edge of the wood line. She wasn't coming out and I was running out of light. It was still light enough to aim and I had a clear shot of her shoulder, so I took the shot. I knew the second I pulled the trigger that it was a good shot and that she was down. My exit from the scaffolding must have looked like a dismount from the uneven bars in gymnastics! (Never mind that the uneven bars is a girls event). There was nothing remotely dignified about the way I ran over to the downed deer. I was too excited to care! Dignity returned when I made it to the animal. I have to tell the total truth; it was a hung jury as far as how I felt... On the one hand, I had finally done it and I was elated; but I and I alone was responsible for the dead animal that now laid on the ground before me. It didn't feel quite the way that I thought it would. There was a somberness about the event. Truthfully, that same emotion has been present every time I've taken an animal since then and quite frankly, if it ever goes away, I'll quit hunting. For me, from that first shot right up until now there is no joy in the kill for me, the joy is in the hunt. Don't mistake my words, I was happy all right! I was happy that the hunt ended in success. But I was also fully aware that I had ended the animal's life. The Native Americans handled it the best. After the hunt was over and the animal down, they prayed over it. Thanking their great spirit for allowing them to harvest one of his animals. Then they honored the deer and thanked its spirit for giving them both a good hunt and meat to sustain their own lives. In other words, they were happy but respectful!

Uncle Ted would say "The beast is dead... long live the beast."

*Never hunt for the joy of the kill. It should be the joy of the hunt that fills your soul with satisfaction. It's what our ancestors did before us. Hunting to put food on their tables. **Never shoot something if you don't intend to eat it, unless it's endangering you, your buddy or your property! Always be respectful of the animals you are hunting. Remember, you're on their turf.***

BULLS EYE

Now that I had cleaned and hung my first deer in the cooler, I was feeling even more like the hunter that I had set out to become. Having meat in the cooler that I had taken through my own efforts was a new sensation. Suddenly, the whole idea of hunting for my existence had come full circle on me. I could not wait to taste the fruits of my effort. Bwana told me that the deer needed to hang for a couple of days before I cut it up, so wait I did. In the meantime, I was now a hunter. I was more serious about the way of life than ever before. See, it had already changed from a sport to a way of life! I was hooked indeed!

While I was waiting, I may as well do some more scouting and hunting. My wife was out of town for the weekend, so I had a" kitchen pass" as we liked to put it at Balenacre. I went to the church in the woods on Sunday morning, spent time with God and all his creatures (while I hunted). It was cold and crisp, a wonderful morning. I felt as alive as I ever had. About 8:30 there were a few does that wondered into the field where I was hunting. They were about 150 yards away from me. Now prior to the incident with taking my scope off, 150 yards was an easy shot for me. But this wasn't target practice; these were live animals. God's creatures...and after all I was in His church! I didn't feel at all comfortable with that long of a shot since I really hadn't taken a longer shot since "cleaning my riffle." They stayed in the field for about a half an hour, but they never came any closer. I passed on taking the shot! That decision, coming from a novice hunter, was about as "experienced" as it gets. I made the right call, I knew it, and it felt great! I enjoyed just watching the animals as they fed and played in the field. It was every bit as satisfying as it had been to take the doe the evening before. Maybe even more so. After they left the field to go and bed down for the day, I climbed down from my stand. I walked back to the cabin with an overwhelming sense of peace. None the less, I knew that I hadn't taken the shot because I was not sure enough about my accuracy at any distance. Obviously, I needed to take some target practice. I went to the shooting range and set up a target, walked back across the dam and set up shop at the bench. I loaded my gun, sat down and got into my shooting position. I pulled up my ski mask and doubled it up on my forehead. I pulled off the first round. It was a little low and left. I chambered another shell and squeezed off another round. It was low and right. OK, was I unintentionally trying to compensate for the first shot or just swaying a bit? Mind you, neither shot was far left or right, and both were about the same in elevation...I tried again, low and right. I unloaded my gun and changed the elevation. Then I reloaded and fired again. Bingo on the elevation, I was still right though. Now for the windage I thought. I corrected for the fact that I had been shooting right, then loaded another round and chambered it. I pulled the trigger and was once again in the "Zone". I pulled a few more rounds off just to be sure. I was really close, but not perfect. I wanted to be at that place where the next time Vernon and I were at the bench together I could indeed place one round right inside another. You know to redeem myself...Male pride and all that. OK, was this the sights or shooter error? I had a moment of brilliance... or so I thought. The best way to check to see

which of the two was the case was to elimi-
nate one of the options. The obvious choice
was shooter error so if I just took my left hand
off the gun entirely and relied on the pillow to
keep the rifle steady, I would know if it was
me or not. Just a reminder, this was the same
30.6 that nobody else wanted to shoot more
than once. You know, the gun Darren had sold
me. The powerful one in the synthetic stock!!!
I squeezed the trigger and got kicked by the
mule! I sat there for a few seconds stunned,
and then said out loud, "that was really stupid!"
And it was! Then I thought "I need to shoot a
few more rounds so I won't be scared of the
gun." I chambered another round and pulled off
the shot. As I started to chamber a third round,
I noticed something wet around my forehead.
I put my hand up to wipe it from my eyes...it
was blood. OK, one more quick round and I'll go
check it out. I shot again... more blood, I pulled
off the doubled-up ski mask and a fountain of
blood spurted across the bench... **"HURT"** I said
in acknowledgement of my "shooter's error". I
stood up from the bench, left everything where
it sat and started for the cabin with the ski
mask pressed against my head. By the time
I got to the cabin, which wasn't far away at
all, the ski mask and my jacket were covered

in blood. There was an old towel by the door that we used to wipe off, well everything that we didn't want in the cabin. Not exactly sanitary, but I didn't want blood in the cabin either. I still felt like I would be able to hide my stupidity. (I hadn't seen my forehead yet.) There would be no hiding this one. There was a perfect bloody circle right between my eyes. And this...through a doubled-up ski mask. I guess you could say "BULLS EYE". Or, you could say YOU IDIOT! To this day I still carry half of the circle in the form of a scar. At least I still have both my eyes.

At the risk of overstating the obvious...***Never, I repeat, never shoot a high powered riffle without having both hands firmly on the gun and the stock firmly against your shoulder.***

When you are making corrections on your scope at the riffle range, always make sure that the gun is unloaded.

*If you're not sure that you can fairly take an animal down with one shot, for any reason, then **don't take the shot**. You owe the animals that much.*

*Once again, I give an example of "Hunt for the hunt, not the kill". **You don't have to pull the trigger to have a fantastic hunt!** I felt better walking away from the field that morning,* *knowing I had done the right thing than I would have felt if I had taken a great buck.*

Lost In Space... Er... Ah The Barrel Field

One Saturday, I felt froggy and jumped up on old blue to brush hog the barrel field so that the clover beneath the chewed-up crops could come in better. The barrel field was so named because of the stand that was situated on one side of it was shaped like a barrel. It was yet another example of original names for the fields or stands at Balenacre. When I finished that afternoon, Earnest informed me that it was usually a good bet to be in a field where you had been cutting up crops or even cutting up dirt. He said the deer could smell the freshness of it all and usually would come in and check it out. I took his advice at face value and after I cleaned up, I headed back out to the barrel field for my evening hunt. As dusk approached, a nice sized doe appeared at the far edge of the field. It was about 120 yards away. I continued to watch her hoping that a buck would follow her into the field. It wasn't a buck that was trailing her, but rather a heavy fog bank. It kept closing in and I'm here to tell you it was so thick it looked like a brick wall. With only moments before the fog enveloped her, I was faced with a shoot her or nothing situation. I chose the former. No sooner than I shot her, she took off in a wide circle that eventually led her into the fog bank. I knew that I should wait, but I also knew that it was a perfect shot and didn't think she would go far. I went across the field (as best I could in the fog) to the point where she was hit. As I thought, I immediately found good sign that she was well hit. The problem was that I couldn't see to follow the blood trail. Basically, I was left groping in the dark, walking around in circles hoping to trip over her or make her eyes glow in my flashlight (that was another trick that I had learned). I was so engrossed with the task of finding my deer that I barely noticed Earnest when he joined me in the search. We continued to do laps and figure eights until I heard Earnest say..." You shot that doe so hard that she grew nuts!" He had found my deer; unfortunately, I had made a classic error. The combination of dusk, distance and the fog closing in had been enough to hide the but-tons on top of the young buck's head. "When you're taking does that happens from time to time" Earnest assured me. "Thanks" I said not really feeling any better. I had passed on so many four pointers and six pointers only to shoot their younger brother. I grabbed the buck's hind legs and started to drag him the short distance back to the cabin. "Where the heck are you going" drawled Earnest. "Back to camp" I answered as I kept dragging. "Not that way you ain't". "Tha cabins over yonder" he said pointing the other way. The combination of doing circles in the fog, the lack of visibility and the disorientation of being in such heavy fog had gotten me completely turned around. I was lost in a field that I had just brushed hogged that afternoon, less than two hundred yards from the cabin. I prepared myself for the "ribbing" I was about to get for the next few weeks. I wasn't disappointed!

I have found Earnest's advice to be true. Deer can't seem to resist the smell of fresh cut crops or turned over dirt. Those options are a good place to hunt.

It can be a good idea to harvest does. Doing so helps to keep the herd from over populating. It also helps to grow bigger bucks if the buck to doe ratio is closer to even. It is also true that when trying to harvest does, it can be hard to distinguish between a doe and a young button head. **A good trick to learn is that does have a rounder forehead than do bucks. Also, while the size of a button head buck and an older doe may be identical, if you look for signs of age in the doe you will be able to see the differences. An older deer will usually have a sway back, and a pooch belly.**

Never allow the approach of inclement weather to decide whether you take a shot. Be it fog or rain, **if you shoot because it's on its way, you risk not being able to find the animal you shot at and that is unacceptable**. The only possible exception to that rule is snow. **If it's not too heavy,** snow can actually make tracking an animal easier.

As the season progressed further, I continued to learn more about hunting, scouting and the outdoors in general. The other guys did their part in taking the rookie under their wings by helping me with my hunting skills. I owe each of them a debt of gratitude for their help and for their friendship. Once again, it was Vernon leading the charge when it came to my education. He began to show me more about being a woodsman. I loved every minute of it. Anything and everything to do with the outdoors was part of the lesson plan. I began to see that hunting was just a sideline to his real passion. And those "useless facts" that interviewer had said he had "such an uncanny ability to store" was a treasure trove for a novice woodsman like myself. But the more he taught me about nature, the more it could be applied towards hunting...and vice versa. I was beginning to get it.

The weekends where the whole gang came out and stayed at the cabin were my favorites. We would all hunt every morning and do various things during the day. We would scout, do farm work or watch football or the occasional archery contest. Those were almost always the source of another ribbing because of my bow. The guy's all had high dollar high tech bows and I had the caveman's bow. I was just as accurate as they were with theirs, but that didn't matter. Jey claimed, "that thing is so slow you could shoot it, set it down and walk up to the target to pull your arrow out about the same time that it hits the target!" "Yea" I came back "then I can stand the target back up after I knocked it down." It was true; the old Pearson did have a lot more knockdown power than the newer bows. Anyway, we'd go out to the field again in the afternoon for a second hunt. With all of us hunting the odds of success were even greater. Success was not measured in whether you yourself got a deer, but rather if any one of us was fortunate enough to harvest one. It was all the same to us. Then we would all meet back at the cabin, cut up, turn up a few cold ones while I cooked some grub (my other nickname was cookie.) We'd play some poker cut up some more turn in and get up the next morning and do it all again. As far as I'm concerned, that's what hunt camp is supposed to be. Good friends', good times, and good grub! Everyone was doing their part to make the weekends "successful". Everyone had taken a nice buck that season including Vernon's son, Justin. Everyone that is except me. I really hadn't noticed it. I was so caught up in the whole big picture that I didn't seem to care what the "score was" it was a great game and that was all that mattered!

A successful hunt camp is based on good friendships. There can't be harmony if petty jealousy exists. When one hunter is successful, all in the camp should be happy for and with them. You can share information with one another and that helps everyone. ***Besides it's just more enjoyable! "I was more*** *caught up in the big picture than in keeping score" ...20 years later that statement rings true. I had it right as a rookie. It's companion- ship, woodsman ship and nature that make a successful hunt camp!*

Which Way Did He Go?

At this point, it had hold of me bad! All I could think about was hunting and being out-doors. My poor wife Dianne was a "hunting widow" and that was all there was to it! The next weekend found me with Vernon, Joe and Jey. It was perfect timing because this was to be the weekend. Friday night turned out to be "hurry up and get off work and find a quick place to hunt" night. Nothing much transpired that night. We all came back in from our per-spective hunting spots, hit the cabin, opened a cold one and started in to cutting up while the "cookin" happened. Now it should be said that the cooking was not a chore. I loved every minute of it. By this time, wild game of every type was being brought out to the camp to be served up. We're talking elk from Colorado, pheasant from Kansas, duck from Remington farms... sportsman's food. And I was able to create recipes for all these wonders. It was like fantasy land for chefs. And I fancy myself a chef. No one from our camp ever complained. Any way a good night was had by all. The next morning found everyone in front of the sign in board/map trying to figure out where to go. Usually at this point in my hunting life, I sat back and listened to all the knowledge before me. "I'm going here for this reason"... "Well I'm going there for that reason." For once in my life, "shut up and listen" became my mantra. Thank the hunting gods for reason cause I've never been that way about anything else... I promise you! But listen I did and learn because of it I also did. Anyway, that morning Joe was the big hit of the day. He killed a really nice eight pointer out of the creek stand. (Guess why we called it the creek stand?) I helped him drag it out and as usual, I was just as happy about it as he was. The afternoon wasn't any different than any other. We watched college football until it was time to "hit the field". I chose the barrel field. It had become the killing field of Balenacre that year. The crop had really come in well and the clover beneath it was like healthy candy. You couldn't go wrong. No one else choose it so I was all over it for the evening. As the hunt progressed, several deer came into and went out of the field. I just watched and waited to see if some young hot doe would bring Mr. big into the field with her. At the last of shooting light, three deer came into the field. (I should point out that there are two versions to this story;) Mine which makes some sense but lacks "comic relief", and Vernon's which is a little less factual, but is much funnier. Actually, both are true, but Vernon's version comes from his ears via the mouth of a hunter who was, shall we say, "a little bit excited". My version first, since it was my hunt.

"These three deer came out into the field at the last possible shooting light" I began... Now after my last incident with the spike, I was going to make certain that whichever deer of the three I chose to take it would NOT have any buttons on its head. As I was glassing each of the deer to be certain, the center doe stuck up its head, now I'm looking for tiny buttons and low and behold, she had a very nice eight-point rack! Holy crap, a shooter! I managed not to fall out of the barrel. I was somehow able to regain control of my senses, then calm down (just a bit) and take advantage of the last bit of shooting light I had left. I waited until the doe to his left cleared out of the way and left me with a view of his shoulder, I took aim, held my breath and gently squeezed the trigger.

Just like every hunting video says you're supposed to do. It was a great hit and I knew it! The
trouble was, there were three deer, all scared
and each of them heading in different directions. It was impossible for even the most experienced of hunters to tell which way my buck
went... let alone me. In my, shall we say cur-
rent heightened state of arousal, I felt "pretty
sure", that he was the one who had spun
around and headed back the same way that
they had come from. Well, "sort of"... maybe,
but who could say for sure? When he got to
the field Vern found a slightly confused, but
very excited if not downright overly exuberant
hunter. One who may not have chosen his next
words very well...at that particular moment!

When he managed to get my breathing rate
down to say a "that of a normal person who
was just on the verge of passing out" he asked
me..." What did you shoot?" What I wanted to
say was "Well, when they first came out into
the field" ...Unfortunately for me I think what
came out was more like... "Well at first it was
a doe, and then it was a buck"...or something like that. It would be the start of years of
harassment. Like the one and only home run
of my little league baseball career. The catcher
behind the plate swore that I had my eyes

closed. My moment of glory was over before I rounded third and headed for home. "Mark, was it a buck or was it a doe" asked Vernon? "That's what I'm trying to tell you", I stated, "at first it was a doe, and then it was a buck"! Perhaps the words "I thought" should have been interjected into that sentence at some point. (As Mr. Owl once said when asked about how many licks it took to get to the center of a tootsie pop)... "the world may never know". At any rate, Vernon heard what he wanted to hear, and I tried to say what I was trying to say. The two were worlds apart. OK, that wasn't going where he wanted it to go. The next logical question was, "Mark, which way did he... er... ah, it go"? "Well first he went this way but then maybe he went that way" The answer was obvious...**I needed speech therapy!** Hell, I was babbling. I wanted to say that I couldn't be sure which way he went since all three of them scattered in different directions, but my tongue just wouldn't cooperate. So, I just jammed the shovel deeper in the dirt and kept digging. Once again, Vernon was beginning to tremble...and once again, my ears were beginning to turn red. The "Wokie" was getting upset again.

We could find no blood at the point of the shot and there was no sign in the direction that I "thought he went in" but Vernon knew, excited or not that I was sure of only one thing... I had just shot my first buck. We looked for over three hours. This wasn't anything at all like the tree killer incident. Vernon knew it as well or he wouldn't have kept looking with me. If he didn't know anything else, he knew that by this point in time, if I had my crosshairs on something with my 0.6, you didn't want to be that "something"! I don't miss! He very calmly said "Mark, let's quit for the evening, I know you hit the buck...we're just not gonna find him tonight. It's plenty cold so he won't go bad, we'll find him in the morning." He was just positive enough so that I knew he believed me, no matter how excited I had been. Or maybe he believed me because I was that excited. It was a long night. I'm not sure how much or if I slept. We got up the next morning and Vern acted as if nothing was different from any other morning of hunting at the farm. "Where are you going" he asked me? "Are you crazy, I'm going to look for that buck" I said. "Why, he's not going anywhere," said Vernon. "Just go hunting like you normally would and we'll find him afterwards once the sun's up good."

"Well, if you say so, that's what I'll do." I went to the white seat. The reason why, was because it was close to the barrel field. And the name, well... the seat was white. Maybe an hour or so after first shooting light this jerk comes walking right up through the woods towards my stand. Wait a minute that was no jerk, it was Vernon. He knew better than that. Heck he had taught **me** better than that, so I knew he knew better. "What in the heck are you doing" I asked him as he got closer? He answered my question with one of his own." Have you been saving your money", he asked? Now I'm thinking, "uh oh, maybe that buck wasn't as big as I thought and I'm gonna get fined"! "I hope so" he continued, "cause taxidermy work ain't cheap". "You found him" I exploded? "Yea, but he didn't go the way you thought" he countered. Well, I slid down the bat pole as fast as I could and off we went on the short trip to the barrel field to look at my buck. We were about halfway through the woods when it hit me what time it was. "Did you even go hunting" I questioned my friend? "It came to me in the night", he said "I knew where he went. You said one of the other "does" went straight across the field." "Yea" I said, "so what?" "Mark, there is a major trail in back of that field that leads to our sanctuary." That was the very first time that I had ever heard that word, but I let it go given the moment. The hit buck ran straight to the safest place on my property, and that's where I found the first blood. In fact, lots of it. It was a good hit alright; you knocked his heart right into the exit wound. That's why there wasn't any blood at the spot where you hit him. We walked ten feet past the edge of the field, right near where I had shot the spike in the fog bank. There was blood sign everywhere. Vernon told me to follow it and I'd find my deer. I questioned my friend again, "you didn't go hunting this morning?" "No, I didn't" he said. "Not with an animal on the ground that needed finding!" "But I would have gladly helped..." I didn't need to finish my sentence. I realized that he wanted me out of the way so he could find the buck without me walking all over sign. He sent me to "my neutral corner" so he could do what he did best. I followed the sign to my buck. He was beautiful. I just stared at him for a minute. I didn't dare look back at my buddy because I knew my eyes were all teared up. For all I knew, his might have been too, he wanted this for me as badly as I wanted it for myself! What a great moment and I had shared it with a great friend. It's a memory that'll never go away.

Weather it comes in the sophisticated form of Professor Higgins having Eliza repeat that "the rain in Spain stays mainly in the plain" with a book on her head, or the slightly rougher version of Barney Fife having Earnest T Bass sayin "hoow doo youu doo Misses Wyyliee"... There's nothing wrong with a little speech therapy now and then... Even if or...especially when you're excited, **think before you speak. Say what you mean and mean what you say.**

Always try to watch the animal you've shot after its hit. Try to follow it to the last line of sight there is and then mark the place where it disappears from sight in your memory banks. Sometimes that's the first place you'll find blood.

If you're sure of a good hit, don't a let lack of sign at the point of impact discourage you from looking for the animal you shot at. **Sometimes it takes quite a bit of distance before the blood finds its way out to where it can be seen.**

The barrel field is referenced many times in this book as the field of choice. A lot of deer have been harvested in this field. There is a reason for that. If you'll remember, Vernon said "there's a major trail in back of this field that leads straight to **"The Sanctuary."** *That* **was the first time I'd ever heard that term. A**

Sanctuary is a vital piece of the QDMA puzzle on any hunting property. Its proximity to the field is what has always made the barrel field such a hot spot. If the deer herd doesn't have some place that they can go to feel safe, then it will find another place to live.

That was the first and the last time that I have ever had to leave an animal on the ground for the night and not gotten up the following morning and immediately started looking for it again. **If you've got one down or even if you think you might have one down but aren't sure, you have no right to go hunting the following morning. Your duty to the animal and to your fellow hunters and to yourself is to make every attempt to locate the animal in question. PERIOD!**

Scampilini!

As the season was beginning to wind down, I was given the "seal of approval" from Vernon's lovely wife Johan. She agreed that since Vernon had to work and since he had promised their son he could go hunting, that I could take Justin out to the farm with me to hunt. Whenever a **good** parent entrusts another adult with the responsibility of watching over their child, it should be considered high praise. However, when that responsibility also involves firearms, and hunting safety...well, that's truly an honor. Justin was a well-educated and responsible young hunter. He had the same teacher as I did. I was now a well-educated and responsible "older" hunter. They both knew that I was good with kids. They also knew well enough by now that I knew safe hunting practices. They had been instilled in me by the entire group at Balenacre.

In short, they both knew that their son would be safe with me.

I picked Justin up early in the afternoon. He already had all his gear packed and ready to go. To say he was pumped would have been a major understatement. We were both primed for a great adventure out in the woods. We loaded up the gear in my truck said goodbye to his mom and then we were off to the races. We yammered on and on about everything from school, to soccer, to girls and oh yea, hunting for the whole trip out to the farm. Towards the end of the trip, I targeted the conversation more towards the hunting aspect. Primarily, I wanted to talk about this hunt and the rules of engagement. I would see him to his stand. We would both settle in our stands and then hunt until legal shooting hours were over. If either of us shot, the hunt would be over. I would then come to his stand and signal him. He would acknowledge my signal and we would go retrieve our prize together. Safety first and all that.

I let him pick the stand that he wanted to hunt out of first. He asked my opinion (which felt good) and we talked about it. We concluded that the barrel field was still seeing lots of action and would probably be his best choice. The barrel itself would also provide lots of good cover for any "extra movement" on his part as well as being the safest platform on the property for him to use. One other advantage of the barrel was that it would provide him with an excellent shooting rest from which he could make his shot. I went to the shot gun field which was named due to its proximity to the cabin. It was close enough that the original stand (which faced the cabin) had been deemed too close to it for anything but a shotgun. The stand had since been relocated so that it was not directly facing the cabin, but the name remained the same. The whole point exactly. Justin and I were both close to the cabin, yet far enough away from one another to also be effective for our hunting purpose. Since we would be facing different directions, we would be safe as well.

I had deer on me from the get-go but wasn't planning on taking the shot unless my second buck for the season showed up. I was confident that Justin would also be seeing deer in his location. I wanted all my focus to be on making sure he had a successful hunt. It didn't take too much longer after that, which was good because my resolve to not shoot was being put to the test by all the action I was seeing. Truth be told, I was enjoying myself immensely just watching all of God's beautiful creatures grazing in the green field over which the sun was casting its amber glow, when BAM! Justin took his shot. I quietly pumped my fist in the air in celebration. Then I let out a couple of dog barks that sent all the deer in my field flying so that I could get down without educating them to my presence. I gathered up my gear, lowered it down from my stand with my rope and swooped it up and headed off to the barrel field to get Justin and see what he had shot. I approached from the back of the stand and gave the recognition signal. He responded and acknowledged that the hunt was over. He opened the door to the box stand and was smiling from ear to ear. "I got her with one shot!" he bellowed. "I heard" I responded. "Congratulations" I said, "Do you know where she went?" "Yea" he said, "she went to the right towards the woods." "Did you hear her crash" I asked him. "I think so" he answered. "Well let's go find her" I said. He unloaded his riffle and climbed down out of the stand. Then he reloaded it and said, "OK let's go find her!" I allowed him to lead to see what he did. He went straight to the point of impact (just like he was supposed to) so far so good. He looked back at his stand to get his orientation right, and then he began to search the ground around the area for sign. "There's some fur" he said excitedly, "and there's some blood" he said with even more excitement in his young voice. "And there's more blood" he began to follow the blood trail like a champion. "Here's the place where I lost sight of her" he announced to me as he looked back to see my smiling face right behind him. "There she is, right over there" he shouted loud enough so that the hunters in the next county would also be able to find her! We went to her and checked to be sure that she was not still alive. He instinctively changed modes. He went from exuberant to respectful just as I had learned to do. I stood by and gave him his earned moment with his deer. He nudged her to make sure she was dead, then unloaded his rifle and knelt beside her. All this without me ever saying a word. The kid knew as much about hunting as I did. Why shouldn't he, he was trained by one of the best. He looked back up at me, the excitement returning to his eyes ..." Let's go get the four-wheeler" I said. We did, and I let him drive us both back to his kill. We loaded her up together and headed back to the skinning post. I helped him hang her up and watched silently as he started to work on cleaning her. He was doing a good job of it, but every once in a while, he would look back over his shoulder at me (just like his father had done). He wasn't doing it to make sure I was paying attention and learning, his eyes were silently asking "am I doing it right"? Whenever he did, I would silently nod my approval of the job he was doing. I had learned "that part" of the lesson from Vernon well. That seemed to be enough for him and he would go back to work. It was one of those magical moments in life. Just then he broke "the spell". He looked back at me and said like any growing boy would, "I'm hungry! What's for dinner?" "You're working on her" I stated. "Do you know how to cut the tenderloins out of her" I asked. "I think so" he answered. I helped him with that and gave him "HIS SEAL of APPROVAL". "You go on and finish her up and I'll get started with your dinner" I told him. He looked proud as a rutting buck that I was going to allow him to finish the job on his own. What he didn't seem to realize was that the window to the kitchen sink where I would be working was only twenty feet away from him. As far as he was concerned, I had told him that he was man enough to finish the job on his own.

I watched him from my perch in the window as I worked on dinner. When he got her hide off her, I quietly came back outside and helped him carry her into the cooler and hang her up. "When are we eating" he asked breaking yet another "spell". "Soon I answered him, wash up and you can help me out." He did, and we worked on the tenderloins he had cut out of his own deer together. "What's this called ", he asked about the meal we were preparing. "It's called scaloppini" I answered. I finished cutting the loins and gently breaded them while he cut up mushrooms for the sauce that we would be making to go with the feast. He worked on his projects, and I worked on mine. We made a feast together out of his fresh kill. Indeed, it was a magic time for both of us. As I stated in the preface of this book, "to take down an animal, prepare its meat and then transfer it into a feast with 'our' own hands, was turning into one of the most fulfilling experiences of 'our' lives." We then set the dinner down in front of us on the huge table. We gave thanks and then dug in. "DUG IN" what an understatement! Now I've got an appetite for good food, but this kid was going at it like a starving kitten. He was giving out all the proper signals that Emily Post would require of a young man enjoying his meal... You know mumming between bites, sopping up gravy with his bread, hovering over his plate going back for seconds, thirds...I was thankful that he wasn't a Bedouin. He didn't burp... or fart, but man did he enjoy the meal that he killed and helped to prepare with his own hands. Man did he! We polished off every bit of the food we had made, cleaned up our mess and sat down to watch Jerry McGuire, one of the movies we had at the cabin. (I'm now totally sick of that movie because we had watched it so many times.) "Man, that was good" he said as he rubbed his full belly. "I mean really good! Thank you" he said. "You're welcome" I said, "but it was your deer, and you helped to prepare it, so I thank you as well". I think at that very moment he got it! Sure, it was a great meal, but the fact that he had been responsible for harvesting that meat and helping to prepare the feast to follow was what made it a truly memorable meal. Justin has loved to cook ever since.

We watched the movie, made sure it ended the same way (it did) and then we went to sleep. After lights out, I heard from his bunk across the room, "that was sure a great meal" I had to agree. "It was a great day", I countered him.

"Yea, that's what I meant too, it was a great day, thanks!"

I thought, "Top *that* for a thank you note, Emily."

We got up the next morning and hunted again but saw no deer. We followed our safe pick-up routine after the hunt was over, went back to the cabin dutifully filled in the log-book we kept and then cleaned up the cabin. We lastly went out and checked on Justin's deer, made sure the cooler was working properly and then went through the close-up procedures for the cabin, locked up and went home. We chitted and chatted about different things on the ride home but, neither the experience... nor the meal came up. "It's hard to tell what makes an impression on a kid" I thought. Maybe he had missed the big picture. Oh well, I didn't miss it and I was sure that there would be other chances for him to get it.

When we arrived at his house, I helped Justin gather up his things. We carried them inside and he went about putting them where they belonged. "Thanks" said Johan to me while he was putting away his stuff. "My pleasure" I told her, and it truly was. Johan told me later that after I had gone and he was finished with his chores, Justin came bounding down the steps and exploded out..." Mom, we had **"*scampolini"*** or something like that for dinner! We made it from the deer that I shot, and it was great! I mean <u>really </u>great!" "I guess it did make the same impression on him that it did on me" I thought to myself as we laughed about her story.

Later I would share the events of the hunt with the kid's father. Especially the part about how he went to the point of impact and blood trailed her using all the right techniques without me ever having to say a word to him. I relayed his respectful attitude, the way he cleaned the doe, all of it. I could tell that Vernon was proud. But like me, he seemed to take the most pride if the fact that his son understood what it meant to be able to fend for himself. That was **"his"** meat that **"we"** had put on **"our"** table. **It truly is a great way of life**. I only wish that my feeble words could attempt to do it justice for those of you who, for your own reasons will never know the sense of inner gratification to one's soul that this "way of life" can provide. It's not about killing at all. It's about doing what we were originally made to do. Provide for our-selves and our family. Not by doing the old nine to five that we've become accustomed to, and then going to the grocery store where a "proxy butcher" did our work for us. But by actually gathering our own meat, that we took with our own hands and turning it into a feast for the ones we love. That's what hunting is all about!

If you are ever lucky enough (and I do mean Lucky enough) to be given the opportunity to teach a novice hunter **something new,** *then please be responsible. Show that person how to be safe. Show them how to be fair and respectful to the animals and show them a good time. That may be the only chance you have to make an impression on them. It may also be the only time that they are ever given the chance to learn what this lifestyle is all about.*

The hunting side of the Justin story does not fully count in the way of teaching a novice about hunting, because at the time he was almost as knowledgeable as I had become. Rather than repeat the whole hunting together scene again and putting it **all** in *italics* and **bold print** in order to highlight the lessons, I would ask you now to go back and read the hunting part of that story again. It's that stocked full of valuable safe hunting practices. If you are showing a new hunter the ropes, then please don't fail to point out to them ahead of time what I did not have to point out to Justin. He had already been shown things like unloading his gun only after he knew his deer was dead. The fact that I was able to observe him doing it right the first time should be used to reiterate how important it is that they are aware of these practices. He was my first experience with teaching, and all that work was already done for me. You probably won't be that fortunate so take the time to show them.

We talked about our hunt. Planned our hunt together and hunted our plan!

*The human-interest side of the Justin story is another matter. It was somewhat related in that it all has to do with the hunting lifestyle. We both learned a valued lesson together. I had been hunting for a couple of years, and I had been cooking wild game for a fair part of the second year, but I had not fully recognized the correlation between the two. Perhaps I should rephrase that. I failed to recognize the **significance** of the correlation. That is what sank in that evening. With this lifestyle, one can enjoy a passion for the outdoors; experience the unmatched feeling of fending for oneself, and the exuberation of creating a delicious meal from that foraging experience. The excitement that Justin was trying to relay to his mother over how good the meal had* *been, was really* **excitement over how good it felt to make a meal that he had taken with his own skills and helped to prepare with his own hands.** Until you've done that, be it through farming, fishing or hunting...I don't think I have the writing skills to fully make you understand how he and I felt. The best I'll ever be able to do is to try and describe it.

Please remember that I was in the refrigeration industry. I have seen with my own eyes the way "that meat" under the plastic wrap met its end. There's nothing fair about it. No one will ever be able to convince me that the animals waiting 'their turn' don't know what's going on. Their scared and that fear turns into adrenalin. That adrenalin then turns into cortisol, a known carcinogen. And then we eat it. One day I would love to get to the point that all the meat that my family ate came from animals that I hunted, but who has that kind of time. And like most of us, I'm going to eat meat. I'm not hypocritical enough to say that I won't eat meat from the grocery store because of how it was taken. I'd just rather kill the animal myself and know how it was done, than to hope that whoever killed it for me was nice about it. I know for a fact that our way of taking an animal is much more humane. The animal has a chance. In fact, it has a much better chance of surviving than we do of taking it. When we do take it, (providing that it's done correctly) that animal never knows what hit it. Not to mention the fact that our animal has not spent its life in a cage or a pen lying around in its own feces. Surely that can't be fairer to the animals. It also can't be healthier for us to ingest!

GRAND OPENING

The last good hunting story that I can remember for that first "real" hunting season involved me hunting alone in a section of woods that nobody else had been hunting. I had done some late season scouting trying to find out where the deer had seemingly disappeared to. The signs that they were leaving seemed to be mainly in this one section of unexplored woods. At least it seemed unexplored by us humans. I took down one of the old unused ladder stands on the property and relocated it to this newly found spot. I felt like an explorer going through virgin territory. "I must be getting really good" I thought. "No one else knew enough to put a stand in here". I congratulated myself on the brilliance of my outdoorsman ship. Now other than the tree fort I built on my own property; this was the first time that I had actually put up a tree stand that I was going to hunt. Once again, I found myself in the dangerous territory of trying to figure it out for myself. Like a muscle-bound gorilla, (all brawn and no brain) I carried the intact 20-foot ladder stand to the spot that I had picked out. It was a place where I figured that the deer would be crossing during daylight hours. It had been easy enough (although dangerously stupid) for me to get the ladder stand down out of the **old dead tree** it had been in. I just climbed up it "carefully" cut the rotted straps from the tree. I then tied a rope to the stand and circled the tree it was in. I tied another rope to the front of the stand and climbed back down. Now all I had to do was grab one rope and pull the stand out away from the tree. I used the one wrapped around the tree to control the stand down to the ground. It was effective but foolish. That part of the plan had worked flawlessly and I wasn't even bleeding. Now I needed to figure out a way to put the stand in its new location without getting banged up in the process. If ever there had been a time for a camera man to be filming for America's Funniest Home Videos that would have been it. A Camera man is exactly what I needed. Well, any kind of a man... a second set of hands, you know some help! I tried a half a dozen or so attempts at getting the stand up. Each of which ended with the ladder crashing back down as I ran for cover. I finally managed to get the thing leaning against the tree. I don't know why, but the thought of giving up never seemed to cross my mind! Anyway, there it now leaned. All I needed to do was climb up it and attach the ratchet strap around the tree and tighten it up. Just like that Christmas present being put together that was mentioned in the forward... there was an extra part that was in my humble, er...ah...stupid opinion, was "unnecessary". If I'd had a manual...wait, I wouldn't have read it if I did have one. Besides all that, the manual might have called the unnecessary part a ladder brace. (This would not be the last of my stories that have to do with this particular part.) Any way, I was about halfway up the ladder stand to tie it off when the ladder started to bend. I, ah... "jumped" yea that's it I jumped to the safety of the hard ground, and then once again ran for cover as the stand once again came crashing down. Kiddies, never confuse persistence...which is a good thing, with stubbornness which is not necessarily a good thing! I rubbed my head (and a few other places) and thought about it for a minute. I then placed my now u-shaped ladder between two trees and straightened it out.

Next, I walked er...limped back to the old stand site and got the "extra" part. I went through the whole process of erecting the ladder stand yet again, and this time I used the unnecessary part just for the sake of argument. What do you know, it worked! I finally left what had been up to that point the relatively undisturbed parcel of woods for the evening to "let it calm down". Since I had never put a stand up before, I didn't know anything about flagging tape or bright eyes or any other way of helping me to find the stand in the dark. The next morning it was, well, dark! There I was in the dark trying desperately to remember where I had placed that new u-shaped ladder stand. So much for stealth, I had flashlights going in every which direction looking for some sign of the missing ladder stand. If someone had been passing by, they would have thought that it was a Grand Opening for a new Wal-Mart or something.

For some reason, my scouting efforts had not panned out the way I thought that they would. Believe it or not, even with all the sign that I had seen while scouting, I didn't see a single deer that morning. Oh yea, and that parcel of woods that nobody else in the hunt club seemed to know about...I think I've used this phrase earlier in the book somewhere...ah sanctuary, yea that was the word, it was our *sanctuary*!

It is both common courtesy and in some cases, it can be a written law that whenever you are putting up a tree stand for hunting purposed on someone else's property or on public land that you **ask permission from the landowner or game warden if it's public land.** You never know there may be a reason why they don't want permanent stands or even hunters at all in certain locations. By not asking, you may be breaking the law, or you may risk losing your hunting privileges on a certain property.

In this case, if I had asked Vernon for permission, I would have been told that the area with all the great sign was devoid of hunters for a very good reason. It was our deer's **sanctuary area**. That is a common Q.D.M.A. practice for better heard management. **(And it works)** The **idea is that for every piece of property that is used for hunting purposes, there should be an area where the deer can go to feel safe, unmolested, and in all ways free from human intervention. Protected! A Sanctuary.** It absolutely makes sense. Once the hunting season is in full swing, the local deer population goes on high alert. They will continue to avoid and otherwise move away from human contact. If *that goes unchecked, they will move right off the property that you are trying to hunt.* **So, by not giving up some part of your property to them you are denying them their own space and they will ultimately leave! Then what are you going to hunt?**

There are whole books written on nothing more than safe practices for erecting stands for hunting. Don't be like me, **READ THEM!** *Every new stand has safety instructions. They're included right there in the price!* **READ THEM!** *Most of the better new stands also come with a safety harness. Again it's included in the price. They too have instructions,* **READ THEM!** *"Repeat the sounding joy", if its Christmas time, "Stirring and stirring and stirring our brew" if it's Halloween, repeating decimals if it's math class, (I'm beginning to see a repetitive thought pattern here, and I hope that you are too.)* **Hundreds of hunters are injured or killed every year in accidents involving tree stands. Most of them are way less stupid than I was. Educate yourself one way or another so that you don't become one of them!**

There are multiple ways to flag or otherwise mark your way back to your hunting locations once you have placed them in the strategic location that you have chosen. Bright eyes are one of the more common types of ways to mark your trail. They are quite simply thumb tacks that glow under the shine of a flashlight. They work great at night but are harder to see during daylight hours. They also sell clothespin types of markers which are orange as well as glow under a flashlight beam. **Place them at about eye level and then when you go to your stand in the early hours briefly turn your flashlight on and "Wally" they will lead you right to your stand.** And they'll do it without the laser light show that scares away all the deer.

That was pretty much the end of my first hunting season with Bwana and the rest of the guy's at Balenacre. As you can tell, the season was fairly uneventful. There were relatively few lessons that were worth mentioning, but at least so far I haven't bored you to death... you're still reading aren't you?

Winter led to spring and since I hadn't caught bird fever (at least not yet) I didn't participate in Turkey season. I did however take part in shed hunting, which was also a new adventure in outdoors for me. Another thing that Vernon turned me on to was hunting for arrowheads. More on that later.

Something else happened that spring. My relationship with the folks at Nichols' Store led me into a contract to do something that I was good at. Darren asked me to help him redesign his deer processing plant. It was a good business deal for both of us and together we took that part of his business to a new level. Now both of us being Southern there isn't much that we like more than a little horse trading. When the business was transacted, part of the payment was in the form of a phat line of credit with which I could acquire some much-needed better gear. It would seem that my earlier statement of "**that's all the gear I would ever need**" was at best a bit erroneous.

Suddenly my middle of the line Simmons came off of my 30.6 and was replaced by a top of the line Burris Euro Diamond. The Simmons, which was still an excellent scope, found a new home on my new Thompson center fire muzzle loader. I also acquired a pair of Steiner "Merlin" 8X42 binoculars, a Leupold RX1 range finder and a Weaver night vision monocular (for scouting). I beefed up my hunting clothing with some Scent Eliminator Camo, and replaced my rubber Wal-Mart boots with a nice pair of Muck Boots. Now I had a good basic start on quality firearms and optics and much better clothing and of course I had my fine bow, which nobody could seem to talk me out of. Although even it was the benefactor of my trading skills. I finally broke down and allowed Darren to sell me those True Fire sights that we had been discussing for over a year. And I also picked up a Whisker Biscuit arrow rest. I was ready! Or so I thought. More famous last words...right?

Working It All In

As spring slowly dragged on into summer, I could finally start to prepare the farm equipment for the summer planting. Once again, I was falling back into my new role as a farmer. I offer my apologies to all of you real farmers out there who feed our country and part of the world with your heroic efforts. I just want to be a part of your world. Something about it has stirred my soul every bit as much as hunting has. I've got a few rookie farmer stories too, though not enough for a book. They'll come up a little bit later. Anyway, we started with brush hogging all the roads. Then we could ride around on the four-wheeler and move trees and logs that were blocking the road. Once that was done, we could get our trucks into the back side of the property for any improvements that might need to be made. It made the jobs of moving stands or repairing them a lot easier. Things like filling salt licks and clearing shooting lanes out so that the stands would be more effective were now possible because we could access the areas via our trucks with ladders, chain saws and pole saws. Wow, hunting... or hunting preparation is hard work. Once again, I loved every minute of it. Well minus the snakes, chiggers and mosquitoes. Why would members of a club want to skip workdays? I would show up with just Vernon and we'd finish some old project or start up a new one. It was Vern's property, but it was our farm! If you can't take pride in someplace, then you don't belong there! Pride is something that I definitely had in Vernon's Place.

Finally, it was time to start planting the fields for the fall harvest. I don't ever remember planting out at Balenace without Joe Stowe being there. Even in the years where for one reason or another he didn't hunt out there very much, he was always there at planting time. I think getting up on his tractor was a way for him to get away from all the responsibility that comes with success. I understood that escape as well (minus the success). It was probably the basis for our bond. Joe and Vernon were both my mentors in the realm of farming.

There were eleven plantable food plot fields at the farm. Not to mention quite a few smaller honey holes that managed to have some seed accidently dumped in them almost every year. The bigger fields all needed to be readied by brush hogging them and then burning them to kill off the grass and weeds. Burning is a very effective way to ready a field but that is only the first step. Before we would burn, we would take the disk around the field to be burned several times. This creates a fire break between the field being burned and the woods. Once done, you go to the upwind side of the field and light it up using a semi-flammable mixture of gasoline and burnt motor oil squirted from a can onto the grass. The oil while it is still flammable helps to take the explosive combustion out of gasoline in its raw form. Once the field has been burned off, and after it's been watched to make sure that the fire is out, you can then disk all the field under and begin the process to ready the field for planting. You want to turn the ground over as well as cut the field up. The idea is to try and cut the ground up so much that it literally looks like fine dirt before you can plant the seed. Then you fertilize the field and plant the designated seed on it. Finally, you drag the field to smooth it out as well as cover the seed over with a fine layer of dirt. The last thing to do is to offer up the farmer's prayer for rain. The right amount of rain. Too little does no good at all and too much will wreck all your hard work.

Burning is indeed an effective way to ready a field for planting, although it is also not a step which can ever be taken lightly! It quite literally involves fire in the woods. That's a dangerous combination if done callously. **The first step in the process is to acquire a burn permit.** Now I've told you that Vernon is a stickler for the letter of the law, but the law is not the main reason why you should obtain a permit. When you call one in, the forest service will give you vital information for a successful burn. The first of that information is where the wind is coming from and in what strength. The last thing you want to have happen is for the wind to flame your fire out of control and into the woods. There are a whole lot of other things that interchange between you and the ranger service, but the last information passed is who you are and where you are, this keeps them from reacting to a false alarm when the smoke is spotted...**and it will be!**

Never try to do a burn with less than three people. That is the bare minimum of "warm bodies" it takes to accomplish it safely. Never try to do a burn without someone who is

experienced at the process. VERY EXPERIENCED! This is NOT a time for on-the-job training!

THE PISTOL FIELD

Finally, all the fields were planted and growing. It was mid-August and in South Carolina, that means the start of bow season. A month before the start, on any given day where the opportunity would arise, you could find me taking target practice with my big bow. Now it took some work getting used to the new True Fire sights that I now had on my bow but once I did, I became incredibly accurate with my bow Just like I was with my 30.06. The new Whisker Biscuit was a hit from the get-go. With it you never have to worry about your arrow moving around as you position yourself for a shot. That had been a problem that I had already run into on another of my failed attempts to draw on a deer.

Shortly after opening day, I had planned to meet my buddy Jey Yates out at the farm for a little r & r and some hard-core bow hunting. We met out there Friday afternoon. We cut up for a bit then we settled down to the business at hand, namely bow hunting. We both stood in front of our sign in board map like it was a Ouija board and attempted to predict the future. "Where will he be O great board"? IDUNNO? seemed to be the only answer it ever gave so we both choose our spots without its help! Jey went to the heart attack stand, while I choose a spot between the big field and to be honest with you, I can't even remember what we used to call that field before this incident... Anyway, the place was called the ladder stand. It was a perfect staging area for deer to come into the field before evening. There were several honey locusts and persimmon trees on which the deer could browse before they moved on out into the field. There was nothing spectac-ular about the stand itself. It wasn't more than fifteen feet off the ground, and there wasn't even a seat. You just had to uncomfortably stand there ready and waiting for the deer to walk by you so you could shoot. There was great cover on both sides as well as behind you but there was no shot from any of those angles. The hunter would have to watch them and when they saw a deer approaching; he would have to go ahead and draw back and then wait for the deer to move into the only shooting lane which was right in front of him. As Jey always liked to say, at that point "you stood out like a terd in a punch bowl!" It never seemed to matter; at least one of us got an unsuspecting deer in that ambush every year. This year, it seemed to be my turn. About maybe four o'clock, I sensed movement in back of me. Three does were moving towards the persimmon trees right in front of me. The wind was coming off my right shoulder and that was the side of the tree that they were passing on, so they were clueless as to my presence. I could now see for myself why this seemingly bad set up had always performed so well in the past. The does were not out in the open yet, and they were focused on getting to the sweet, tasty fruit that the trees bared. I quietly drew my huge bow back and waited. I was beginning to see why everyone else preferred the newer smaller bows. It was not easy to say the least wielding such a cumbersome weapon in such an awkward position. There is also a little thing in bow hunting called "let off". That is the reduced tension on an archer's arms once the bow is at full draw. On the new modern bows, the let off is significantly less once in that position, but remember, my bow had once been owned by Odysseus. It was ancient and if there was any let off of its 100-pound draw weight...it wasn't very much! As I waited for the unsuspecting does to saunter by me at their leisurely pace, my arms began to feel the burn of the tension weight. After about two days... I mean minutes; they finally had cleared my stand. My arms were shaking. It was another week, or so it seemed, before the one that I wanted to take decided to turn so that she was quartering away from me. It wasn't the perfect broadside shot I was hoping for, but it was a good enough for a clean pass through. I settled my sight pin on the back of her vitals so that the arrow would pass through both of her lungs resulting in the quick kill that I was looking for. She was only ten yards away from me so any attempt at stopping her with some kind of noise would only have succeeded in scaring her into the next county. I took the shot at the slowly moving deer. A rookie mistake! None the less, I hit her fairly well. She ran about forty yards and then crashed in the extremely thick briars which were all around the area between the two fields. My first bow kill was at hand! I was beyond excited! I stood in the stand for another ten hours...I mean minutes until I finally couldn't stand it anymore. That's when I made my next rookie mistake.

I very prematurely climbed down out of my stand. I stood there for another minute until my heart slowed to the rate of a marathon runner in their 25th mile. And then I started off after my downed deer. When she had been hit, she ran off to her left in a half circle. The wind was still over my right shoulder and as such was blowing my scent right towards the injured deer. Once that happened, she jumped up and took off through the underbrush where a rabbit would have had trouble going. I realized my mistake immediately, but that was already too late. I quietly left the area and walked back to the cabin. I put my bow up and changed my cloths and prepared to hunt for my downed animal. I gathered flashlights, my machete and a pistol which I had bought the previous Christmas for my wife. She had been handling the cash for Mike's office and I had wanted her to have the gun for her protection. It was a small Smith & Wesson 380, a semi-automatic 38. I thought it was the perfect gift for her, but she hadn't seemed to agree with me. I could barely get her to shoot it a few times. It ended up in my arsenal (unbeknownst to her) as a back-up weapon. I had purchased an ankle holster so that I could carry it in delicate situations. It also made a perfect back-up weapon for bow hunting. While the story of Vernon putting down that deer with his knife the season before had made a wonderful impression on me, I wasn't sure yet that I had it in me to do the same.

I left the cabin still confident that the doe hadn't gone far. I walked back down the road to the site where she had last been. It had been over an hour since I had made my second mistake, so I figured it was time for my third. I went back to the point of impact and picked up the blood trail. I successfully followed it through the increasingly thick briars. I found my arrow. It had pink frothy blood on it. That, I had been taught was the sign of a lung hit, which was a good sign. I continued my search to the point where she had originally crashed. Sure enough, there was a pool of blood where she had fallen. If I had simply waited at my stand, she would have died right there in just a little while. Now I was making the same mistake all over again. My fear was that with darkness approaching, we would not be able to find her in the dark. That was a valid point, but there was still more than two hours of daylight left. The further I followed the doe's blood trail, the more I had to rely on my machete to clear the trail through the briars. The more I hacked away at the underbrush, the more the injured doe moved away from her noisy pursuer. As the onset of dusk came closer, I was not. That is, I was not any closer to the animal that I had shot than I had been two hours ago. It was not from lack of trying. It was from lack of knowledge. Actually, if the truth be told, it was from a lack of using the knowledge that I had already been taught. Shortly after sundown, Jey showed up on the scene. He had been walking down the road next to the field and had followed the sound of my efforts. As I filled him in on the events of the afternoon, I saw the smile on his face over my good fortune turn to disappointment as realization sank in. In my effort to find the deer on my own, I had made the task now before us infinitely more challenging. None the less, and to the big guy's credit, he cheerfully joined in the search. Jey's tracking skills were far more advanced than mine were at the time or even today for that matter. We searched for three more hours through terrain that would make a billy goat puke. It was becoming apparent that the doe's wound had either crusted up, or she was nearly out of blood. There was more of our own blood on the ground at that point than there was of the deer's. Neither one of us wanted to admit it, but it was time to quit. The really tuff part was that it was summer. There was absolutely no way that the deer's meat would be any good in the morning, but both of our flashlights were failing at the same rate as the blood trail. We or rather I should say I had lost her. I was sick! I had gone from the exhilaration of my first bow kill to the accepted knowledge that my mistakes had cost me to lose the animal which I had killed. It was the first time that I had not been able to find an animal after it had been shot. I felt ashamed. Jey truthfully tried to reassure me that that was the way it was sometimes with bow hunting. "Crude instruments like bows can't always be effective" he said. "No matter how careful you are, this kind of thing is going to happen." Trouble was, I knew that I had not been careful. I had made three mistakes in a row and had cost an animal its life for nothing. If I couldn't recover it...well I just felt sick!

We walked back to the cabin almost in silence. Jey would try occasionally, to make some kind of reassuring statement but he wasn't getting through to me. It wasn't until we reached the cabin and I went to unload my pistol (a camp tradition) that I realized that the pistol wasn't in my ankle holster any more. It was gone! Somewhere in the struggle to navigate the briars and bramble bushes looking for the shot deer, I had lost my wife's pistol.

The next morning found me doing exactly what I should have been doing; looking for the deer we had not been able to recover the night before. I went to the spot where we had run out of battery life for our flashlights the night before and started the hunt once again. By midday, the late summer southern sun was scorching hot. I'm sure I took that as my penitence for harming the doe to no avail. I continued slowly on until I was out of the briars and into the woods. I was thankful for that, penitence is one thing, running headlong into a rattle snake when you're on all fours looking for blood is quite another. Moving through the woods was equivalent to being on an escalator comparatively speaking. Eventually, I came to the spot where the deer had finally succumbed to her wound. The coyotes had found her and there wasn't very much left. I had done my duty and found the animal which I had killed, but there was no joy in it for me. I would not even allow myself the satisfaction of being able to trail the deer to completion. The time for patting myself on the back would have been if I had stayed put in my stand the night before. Uncomfortable though it was, staying put would have allowed the doe to die in the spot where she had first crashed. I back tracked to the starting point for that morning and began the futile search for Dianne's pistol. We all took turns throughout the season trying to locate that gun. The next season we even burned the field of briars and plowed the field. Nothing ever turned up. The only thing left to do was to rename that field "The Pistol Field" We searched for years for that gun, it was never found. Perhaps one day far in the future some archeologist will find it and put it in a museum. I just hope they will not be able to recover its origin or how it ever came to be in that field.

You should avoid, if at all possible, ever taking a shot at a moving animal. Even if you regularly practice shooting at moving targets, at any given moment, animals can change speed or direction causing a bad hit. A bad hit was not the cause of my unfortunate incident, but it easily could have been.

The main cause of me not being able to recover the animal which I had shot was my inability to contain my own excitement. **After I had taken the successful shot, I did not give the animal in question time to expire. Unless you are in plain sight of the animal that has been hit and know for sure that it is in fact**

dead, always try to give that animal at least an hour before you begin the search for it. For sure that one simple act can make both the animals passing as well as your ability to harvest its meat infinitely easier.

When searching for a downed animal, especially when bow hunting, it is always a good idea to have a weapon of some sort readily at hand. It can be used either to dispatch a wounded animal once it has been found or to defend your prize and or yourself from any predators which try to take it from you. Make sure that it is not illegal in the state that you are hunting in before doing so.

While I am not condoning any of my actions after my hunt was over, I will commend both my own as well as Jey's dedication to finding the downed animal. He and I exhausted every avenue at our disposal that evening in our search. The terrain in which we were conducting our search was far from hospitable and still we continued. **Never leave an animal on the ground without giving every effort to recover it. There are two exceptions to this rule. First if the search places you or your hunting partners in imminent danger then you should stop. Second, if the shot was questionable enough that the animal was certainly not going** *to quickly die. Then sometimes (weather per-mitting) it is best to back out of the woods for the night. This will allow the injured animal to bed down close to the point of impact and hope-fully peacefully bleed out during the night in its sleep.* Immediately begin your efforts to find the animal in the morning. To start a new hunt on a morning after such an event rather than doing your duty to the animal and the hunting community is *ETHICLY AND MORALLY WRONG! Period! GO FIND THAT ANIMAL! No Exceptions! No Excuses! Any Questions?*

This advice is mostly for husbands but can pertain to others as well. Never buy your wife (or anyone else) a pistol no matter how strongly you feel that they need it for their own protec-tion unless they agree with you and are willing to learn to use it. *A gun in the wrong (or inca-pable) hands can do far more harm than good.*

Lastly, it has always been the rule at Balenacre that whenever your hunt is over and before you entered the cabin you unloaded your gun. I can think of no reason why that rule should ever be broken. Not doing so is neg-ligence and such actions are how accidents occur. *Always unload your gun completely, not just the chambered round.*

CHANGE IT UP

As we drew a little bit closer to the gun season, it was determined that some of the stands on the property were going to need to be moved. Why I couldn't be sure. The ones marked for movement seemed to me to be in perfect locations. They were in areas where the topography was exactly what I had been taught that you were looking for when hunting. They were also well concealed. And they were at or near food sources or bedding areas. Yet those who knew more than I did said "move em", so we did.

THE NOSEBLEED STAND

We started with an area that I had really started thinking about earlier in the summer. It was at the back side of the property, about as far away from the cabin as you could get. It was an old clear-cut area with relatively new pines growing as thick as they could get. I had thought as we were working that summer that this might be a good place to explore as a new place to hunt. It turns out that I was right. The other guys had the same thought and were putting it into action. I had missed the day that they originally put the stand up. On the day that I showed up to help, it was already up. And I do mean up. They had chosen the one area in the entire forty acres that had existing trees. It was a funnel of hardwoods that curved off in a semi-circle about halfway into the young pines. Like the disappearing deer field, there was a gully that ran down the tree line on its back side. It ran right down to the tree which they had put the stand in. The ladder to the stand was on the hill which added about six feet to its height in relation to the gully. Once you climbed up the ladder some twenty-five feet up from the hill you looked down at the base of the gully and that added another six feet to the height of the seat. It was up there, but it gave a commanding view of the young pines in which the deer were bedding. In everyone's haste the week before to get the stand up and go hunting, they had not tied the stand to the tree yet. Also, there were some hand hold issues at the top which made for some difficulty in getting seated. Since I had missed the week before when it had been erected, I volunteered to make the adjustments. Twenty-five feet was a bit higher than most of the stands that were on the farm but not all that much, but when I got to the top and made the tricky transition to the seat so that I could finish securing the stand to the tree, the additional six feet down to the gully made me feel like I was in a skyscraper, or the cheap seats at a ball field. You know the nosebleed section. I finished the work and sat down to look for any limbs which might need to be trimmed for shooting lanes. Since none of the pines were over eight feet high, no trimming was necessary. I scampered down the tree and off we went to the next site.

The Koala Stand

The next stand site was a place next to the main road near the big field. Bwana had thought it would be a great stand location. He said it was a great place for deer to stage before coming into the big field in the evenings. "Stage" I questioned "are these deer actors or something?" Jey explained "Staging is the term used for when deer kind of get together and bunch up before they enter a field at twilight." "Oh, yea that staging" I said trying to regain my composure. "Yea right" teased Earnest; "you didn't have a clue what we were talking about." "That's alright" I countered, at least I know the difference between a hammer and a screwdriver!" Earnest was not known for participating on workdays. "Ha ha, very funny" he retorted. "Knock it off you clowns" said Vernon, y'all find a good spot in this section of woods and put the stand up. Joe and I are going to look for some other spots to work on." With that, they left Jey, Earnest and I to erect the new stand. I followed Jey's lead and did the grunt work. He was much better at this kind of thing than me. We finally agreed on the spot and started on the task at hand. Earnest held the base of the ladder while Jey and I walked it hand over hand until it was leaning up against the tree. Remembering that Jey was no fan of heights, I volunteered to scamper up the ladder and put a ratchet strap around the tree. "Fine," said Jey, I'll hold the base of the ladder, "Earnest, you get on the other side and make sure the ladder doesn't bend in since the brace isn't on yet." So that was the plan. Jey held the base in place, Earnest moved around to the other side, and I started up the ladder. I was about two thirds of the way up when the ladder gave way. It bent in towards the pine tree folding the stand part back over my head. Quick thinking and agility on my part is all that saved me from a rough elevator ride to the ground. I jumped from the ladder to the tree wrapped my legs around the trunk and bear hugged it with my arms. "What the hell are you doing," yelled Jey? "Hanging on for dear life you idiot" I yelled back! "Not you Mark, Earnest!" He had wandered off to do some scouting around the area, leaving his job as the human brace left undone. That is why the ladder collapsed. Shouting out threats and obstinacies, I clamored down the pine tree to "rectify the situation." The Wokie was back and ready to tear an arm from its socket! As I reached the bottom (in Olympic qualifying time) Jey was there to stop me. There's nothing like having a Citadel lineman in your way to keep you in line. He quick wittedly defused the situation. "You looked like a Koala Bear scampering down that tree" he bellowed in laughter! I was still hot under the collar and all my fur was standing on ends, but the big guy was tickled and laughing so hard that once again, the Wokie began to see the humor of the whole scene and decided to join in the laughter. I had to admit, if I had been on the ground looking up, I would have found the sight funny. Like I promised you before, once again the ladder brace had shown its importance in erecting ladder stands. About that time, Vernon and Joe came back to show us the next stand location. "What's so funny" Joe questioned? Jey quickly told them the new name for this stand. Joe joined in the laughter while Vernon was forced to take the concerned property owner's stance. He chewed Earnest a new one for shucking his duty and then jumped on Jey for allowing the rookie to go up a tree without a harness. Me he took pity on since the bark from the pine tree that I had a death grip on had skinned my bare arms and legs up badly. After he had done his ownership duty, we all had a really good laugh over the comedy routine that could have turned out much worse.

Any good hunter can and will tell you that repetitiveness can both be a good thing and it can also be a bad thing. It depends entirely on the context of the subject. If for instance, repetitiveness refers to a habit of doing things a certain way every time so that the end result is always the same or at least close to the same, then that is a good thing. Examples of this way of thinking in relationship to hunting might be showering with scent free soap prior to each hunt. That way you're always going into the field in the least offensive way possible. Another might be the trained systematic way in which a bow hunter draws his or her bow in the exact same way to the exact same point every time that they fire their weapon. These are some of the many ways in which doing the same thing the same way every time can and will definitely help you out as a hunter. But what about those instances where doing the same things over and over again can be a detriment to a hunter?

No doubt, if you have talked with, been around or actually been a hunter for a long period of time, then you have heard the phrase of "patterning a deer." Patterning a deer or patterning deer herds refers to a hunter being able to predict what deer are going to do next or where they are going to go or perhaps hide when faced with danger. This is not hocus pocus, or mind reading but rather keen observation and simple animal husbandry. In certain situations, deer will react the same way almost every time, all things being equal. We are animals just like the deer we are hunting. Why then is it so hard to believe that these animals, who are in almost every regard our betters when we are both in the woods, cannot also pattern us as well? The answer is in my opinion quite simple. The only hunters who do not acknowledge that animals can also pattern us are the ones who consistently come out of the woods with does, small deer or no deer at all. Animals rely on instinct and their senses to survive in the forest. Those who do not die young. Those who do are very tricky to catch making the same mistake twice. Thus, as hunters of those cagy old monarchs of the woods we must avoid repeating things when we are in their territory. If we do not, they will avoid us as naturally as a Nascar driver might turn left. Going to your stand at the same time and leaving it at the same time is a way to allow animals to pattern you. Walking to your stand in the same way every time is a sure way to allow deer to pattern you. Using the same stands themselves is another way to get caught. Many times, I have been in a well concealed stand location, as scent free as possible while remaining motionless, had a deer turn the corner heading towards that stand, stop and look directly at me for no apparent reason, and then bolted. Did I do something wrong to alert them to my presence? Well yes and no. No in that I was well concealed, and clean and quiet...all the things that we've been taught to do, and yes that we were simply pegged as to being in the same spot that either I or some other hunter had been previously busted in. The deer simply knew to look up at that spot and determine if there was a danger present. There has been research done which seems to confirm that deer learn to avoid permanent stand sites.

As far as the koala Bear stand goes, never go up a ladder stand to do anything without first putting at least one brace between the ladder and the tree.

If you're working as a team on a project... any project, always do your part of the job. Others are counting on you and the safety of others may very well depend on you.

Always use a climbing harness when you are putting up any kind of a stand that is off the ground.

OLD BLOOD & NUTS

The season seemed to be progressing along fairly slow. No one had claimed any of the large bucks known to have been traveling around on the property. There were some close encounters but none of them resulted in an actual kill. Now about the time of the last week in October, which I think is my favorite time to be in the woods in the south; my other brother-in-law Michael came into town. He and I are close, so I gave him an invitation to come hunting with me, but he was not inclined to pay the out of state license fee. I would have loved to have taken him but no license no hunt. Prior to him arriving, my wife had done some shopping for his birthday present. While she was out, she also picked up a few things for me as well. She is the quintessential thrift shopper and can find deals on any and everything. This time, her talent culminated in her finding a bunch of blaze orange tee shirts which I think she ultimately paid about a dollar a piece for. Now on Michael's birthday, the wind was right, so I had planned on going hunting...which I did! I have learned that there is some kind of phenomenon about friends, family, and guests showing up right when the rut starts to kick in good. The answer is simple...don't let it bother you. Invite them along if you can, if they decline go anyway! **It's the rut!** Anyway, that's what I did, I went hunting.

I had been patiently waiting for the wind to be right for a stand that I had brought back from the dead. It was secluded in the upper quadrant of the north forty in which the Nosebleed had been placed. The stand was located on the opposite side of the bedding area from the nosebleed stand. It was rightly called (in the tradition of all the farm's stands) the Two-Mile Stand. Why you ask...that would be because of the distance from the cabin. Not only was it a journey, the last third of the way was completely inaccessible by four-wheeler. It was the Balenacre equivalent of the Ardennes, I mean it was thick! I reached the stand about 2:30 in the afternoon. I climbed up, then raised up my gear and settled in for the duration. It turns out that I didn't have too long to wait. After about a half an hour's wait, I decided to try my new

Knight & Hale buck call out. I gave a couple of grunts and then waited to see if anyone was at home and wanted to play. It turns out that they were, and they did. From the upper right of the only shooting lane for the stand I began to hear a buck. It was not like any that I had heard on T V. Every two or three seconds I heard a short grunt coming down the line between the clear cut and the wood line. I honestly thought that someone was having fun with me at first. You know, "messing with Sasquatch"! The Wokie in me didn't think that was smart or funny! Then from the right of the five-foot shooting lane came a rather nervous doe. She took a few steps and then looked back over her shoulder at something. That's when I heard the buck grunt again. The doe turned left and trotted off. The buck came into view from the right grunting every time his front hoof hit the dirt. I bleated like the pros on the tube do, to stop him... It worked. He stopped apparently looking around for the other doe in the area. But he stopped with his head hidden by the bushes to the left which marked the end of the shooting lane where the doe had disappeared. I had seen a nice rack as he walked by and it was definitely four points on the side I saw. I knew he wouldn't stay long. It was an easy shot for his vitals. The split-second decision was shoot him...that's what I did. He fell right in his tracks! Now normally that's a good thing, but in this instance, he fell with his head still hidden behind the bushes. He thrashed about a few times and then remained still. I felt sure he was dead, but I wasn't about to ever make that mistake again. I waited and watched his big body for the better part of an hour. He never moved again in all that time. The wait was brutal, he was less than forty yards away from me and I could see all of him but his head! Finally, I deemed it safe to climb down. I lowered my gear down and picked up my riffle, reloaded it and crept towards my buck. I aimed the gun at him and gently nudged him with my boot. He didn't move. He was dead. I somberly gave the animal the respect he deserved, and I thanked God for the great day in the woods He had given me. Then I gave the big guy the once over. He was an older deer by the looks of him. His body was much bigger than the eight I was blessed with the last season but alas, he only had three points on the other side. He was a seven pointer, not the club accepted eight or better. His rack was more than big enough, and he was well outside of his ears... his right side was just undeveloped in relation to his left side. It seemed that I had goofed yet again. Still, he was a beauty and given the quick and only view I would ever get of him, had I not taken the shot, I assured myself that in the same set of circumstances I would have shot again. I would accept my fine like a gentleman and move on.

Now I was faced with the daunting task of getting the 180 lb. buck out of the woods by myself without the use of a four-wheeler. I had helped the other guys, when they were the fortunate ones, drag big deer out for short distances. That was chore enough with two of us pulling for a brief period, but this was a long way, and I was alone. It seemed like a great time for one of those "Inventions" of mine but with no materials around nothing was coming to mind at the moment. It struck me that I was a big beefy guy and that I had carried a lot more weight than that deer around and for longer distances than I would need to go to have the accessibility for a vehicle. I would rather carry him out than drag him. I walked all the way back to the cabin and unloaded my riffle' Then I put my stuff away and changed into a pair of jeans and one of the dollar tee shirts that Dianne had bought me so that I wouldn't end up as someone else's target practice' Finally I grabbed my pistol. My OTHER pistol and jumped on the four-wheeler and drove back as far as I could go. I shut off the quad and walked back to my buck. "The best laid plans" ...well evidently the best laid plans come from somebody else when it involves hunting! I then tried to lift the slightly uncooperative buck onto my shoulders. Now I'm a big man, and in my day, I've been known to throw a fair amount of weight around in a gym, enough to impress most of the people who may have been watching. I was thankful that they weren't around to watch the first attempts I made to throw the beast over my head. I could easily clean and jerk 235 over my head in the gym. The only resemblance in my lift attempts on this buck to that last sentence is the word "dead!" The buck was dead. Period. Nothing else was the same at all. First, in the weight room you always have a spotter. There were a couple of squirrels who seemed interested in my efforts, but they didn't offer to help. I doubted they were strong enough anyway. Next there's the fact that the weight is always attached with collars to a rigid weight bar. I was going to have to wait for several more hours before the buck was anything close to rigid. Patience may in fact be "a virtue", but as you've probably already figured out, it isn't one of mine! This buck was going out of the woods with me! NOW! The final thing missing on this deer that's present in the gym was handles. That weight bar had grips and this deer did not. For my first attempt at 180, I grabbed one of his front legs in my left hand and one of his hind legs in my right hand. I then squatted down, got my legs under me, balanced myself and heaved upwards while throwing the deer up over my head. Yea...right! He went up over my head all right, "over" being the key word in that statement! All the way over my head and behind me with me following right behind him, landing flat on my back. I hadn't counted on the buck flopping around when I went to heave it up. First the legs moved for about six inches before I finally took up the full weight of the buck. That threw my timing off and therefore my balance as well. "OK that didn't work" I said (I guess to the squirrels) "he's too floppy." Next, I tried a less forceful approach. I worked my head under his torso... **alright**, let's not even go there! I'm sure that had to have looked funny, weird, and maybe even a little bit sick. I was attempting to get him on my shoulders before I stood up **OK**? Anyway, that didn't work either. There I was with my head under the belly of a dead deer, and my butt sticking up in the air. The only good that came of the ordeal was the fact that the squirrels didn't seem to have a camera. Not that it matters much since I'm going into such detail about it now. Well at least they're only mental pictures! OK kiddies, remember a while back when we talked about the difference between persistence and stubbornness? A better question might be "do I?" This deer was leaving with me, and I wasn't dragging him. I was carrying him out like Daniel Boone! But even old "Dan'll" would have had his Indian friend Mingo to help him. I tied a rope to his antlers and threw the other end over a branch over my head. Next, I heaved the buck up until he was over my head, then I got underneath him and lowered him back onto my shoulders. I readjusted his weight until I had him balanced and off I started through the woods dragging the rope behind me. I stopped and coiled it up and hung it over his antlers. Then I was off again pleased as punch with myself for doing this the "easy way." Well... now that I had him up, it was easier than dragging him! I was cruising along through the woods at a pretty good pace for a while. Then I hit a hill. Now I wasn't going up or down the hill, I was walking perpendicular to it. I thought that was a blessing but as it turns out it wasn't. The deer shifted on my shoulders in favor of the gravity pulling it downhill. I tried to shift it back into place with a couple of hops which seemed to help some. I started out again. As I walked, I began to feel the sensation of something warm trickling gently down my chest. Like me the trickling was persistent, in fact it grew. The trickle had turned into a stream. A steady stream! I looked down at my brand new, blaze orange, "dollar" tee shirt. It wasn't orange anymore! It was red. In fact, it was "Blood Red". The combination of the deer shifting and me hoping to readjust it on my shoulders had opened the exit wound on the deer and now all that blood was pouring out and all over me! What a mess! There wasn't a thing I could do about it either shy of putting the buck down and that wasn't gonna happen! I just had to endure the misery of the situation until I reached the four-wheeler which was still a long ways off. By the time I got there, I was exhausted and soaked. But I had a nice deer, and I had carried it out of the woods all by myself just like Daniel Boone. I threw the animal on my horse...er..ah..my quad and rode back into camp.

After I cleaned the buck and put him in the walk-in cooler, I called my wife and let her know that I was out of the woods and safe. Then I told her the whole story. Now I can usually tell her the funniest jokes on the planet one after the other and she'll just look at me with a stone face and never crack a smile but this time I had her laughing. Her brother wanted in on the laughter, so she put us on speaker phone as I finished up the story. But when I got to the part about the blood pouring out of the deer and onto my tee shirt all he could say was "that was a brand-new tee shirt. You only wore it once and now it's ruined!" Dianne tried to point out that "it was only a dollar" but that didn't seem to matter. "It's orange (or rather it was orange) so that he doesn't get shot. I'd rather it was the deer's blood on the shirt than his own" she said.

Years later, standing around a campfire Vernon shared this story over a few cold ones with one of our neighbors. We all had a good laugh over it and then Mark, our neighbor whom I barely knew at the time asked me "Mark, when you were carrying this deer, when you looked to the left what'd you see?" "His head I guess," I answered, "why?" "OK" he said, "When you looked to your right what were you looking at"? With that, everyone at the bonfire had another good laugh and I had a new nick name..." Blood & Nuts"

There should be a happy medium between friends, family, and obligations, and your hunting schedule. First of all, remember that very few of us are fortunate enough to actually make our living in the hunting industry. So, you should always make sure that your obligations for work are put before hunting. Passions can become obsessions and obsessions can become addictions. ***Just like a crack head might hit their grandmother over the head for a chance to score some rock, a hunter whose passion has become an addiction may blow off their customers or boss for the opportunity to go hunting.***

As far as friends and family goes, I of course think that family should come first. Your son's football game or a date night with your wife ought to come before an afternoon in the woods. By the same token, these are the people who love you and know you the best. They should be able to understand that you are passionate about this lifestyle and find ways to give you the space to pursue it. ***Even if your passion has become an obsession, make sure that you don't allow it to take the next step... the destructive one, the addictive one!***

Don't rush the decision to go to a particular stand that you're excited about until all the conditions fit into place. All of them! In the instance of the two-mile stand, the whole thing started when Jey and I were out working on stands at the very beginning of the summer. We were near the upper forty and he was telling me about the old stand that used to be there. He said it was a great rut stand because of its proximity to the doe bedding area that was smack dab in the middle of the young pines. He told me no one hunted it anymore because it had become unsafe but that it had produced some monsters before it was discarded. I found it, quietly fixed it up and waited until the rut to use it. There was only one wind direction that worked for the setup, and it was not the predominate wind. That meant I would have to wait on the right wind once the rut arrived. It came on my brother in laws birthday. I had waited patiently for months to use it and now that everything was in place, I wasn't going to waste the opportunity just because it was a special day. I hunted it and my patience paid off in body weight and bone. **When you've got a special stand location, always wait until all the conditions are right before you hunt it. Don't waste all your effort!**

It was years before I found out the answer to the quick grunting buck in this story. I was watching an infomercial about a particular deer call on the Outdoor Channel. The narrator was talking about how when a buck is chasing a hot doe, he will follow her making short grunts about the duration of once for every time his front hoof hit the ground. That is exactly what had happened at the two mile stand that day! Talk about a light bulb going off. I've used the calling sequence ever since.

As far as the segment on taking a buck that was a non-shooter by club standards...Those rules (and they are good ones) are in place to keep people honest. When I told Vernon and Joe about my error and once they had seen the buck in question, they absolved me of any wrongdoing. Joe said "I'd have shot him in that situation. Vernon said "number one, that was an older deer and he was only a seven pointer. He needed to be culled from the gene pool. Number two, given the situation and the amount of time you had to make a split deci-sion, you made a contentious one and thought you were doing the right thing." He gave me an example of abuse of those rules where one member of the club had shot a "four-point doe" ...with a bow! "At a range close enough to use a bow, there was no way that a four-point young buck could be mistaken for a doe. I finned him for taking the shot!" **Club rules are made for the benefit of the club. It's the president's decision as to enforcing those rules. Whatever he says goes.**

There are a number of good products on the market designed to help hunters carry their fresh kills out of the woods without the use of a four-wheeler. It's not a bad idea at all to have one of those on hand, especially if you don't own an ATV. Even if you do own one, it could break down or as it is in this story, the terrain may be so rugged that you aren't able to utilize the quad. **Look into the types and choose the one that best suits your hunting style.**

We always use a sign in board at our hunt club. It helps the other hunters know where you are located so as not to interrupt your hunt. It also serves as a beacon if due to some mishap or injury you do not come out of the woods. **That said, if you happen to be hunting alone, make sure in addition to using the sign in board that you let someone know that you are hunting, where you are hunting and for how long you are planning to be in the woods.** Then make arrangements with that person so that they are expecting a phone call from you once *you are out of the woods. If you don't call, then they know to send help and where to send it.*

The Art Of Game

Over the years I have met numerous hunters who hunt for various reasons other than just for the pleasure of bringing down an animal and enjoying its meat. The sensation of providing for myself and for my family and friends is what does it for me, but everybody's different. Who's to say that my way is right for everyone or that their way is right for me? You know what, I'm gonna take that back. To heck with political correctness, I believe what I believe... unless it's destructive or dangerous, if you aren't gonna eat it, then don't shoot it!

Let's face it, there are people who can't open a can of Campbell's soup and put it in a pan without wrecking it. Some people just can't cook! All of us have had a bad steak or say some chicken that someone cooked on the grill where we're sure that the grill brush (if they even used one) would have tasted better than the chicken. Unless the experience was completely horrifying, it didn't stop us from eating steak or chicken. More than likely, you just chose to decline another offer to dinner at that person's house. Or if, for the sake of manners you could not escape having to "dine" there's always the tactful Christmas cook-book. One can only hope they won't regift to someone who loves to cook and doesn't need it! Why then if someone has served you a com-pletely nasty meal of Venison would you deem "all venison as nasty?" Perhaps it was served by one of those people don't know how to boil water let alone cook. Or maybe the person who served you the indigestible meal just did not know how to properly prepare and then serve venison, or any other game for that matter. We've all known someone who when you offered to create a dining experience for them answered by saying "I don't care for venison." "I had a friend who fixed some for me once and I couldn't even chew it." At one time I felt exactly the same way for the very same rea-sons. Had I not tried to give it another chance, I would be missing out on some of the most delicious meals I have ever enjoyed.

As I have mentioned before, I spent years in the food industry building walk in coolers and freezers. Many of my customers handle various product lines for the meat industry. One such customer of mine and I were discussing his business needs one afternoon. It was just a few days after I had taken the big seven-pointer. He was describing what he wanted from his cooler as it pertained to his process of ageing his beef. He went into a long dissertation about the differences between regular beef and aged beef. All I needed to know was the specifications under which he wanted his cooler to operate. On and on he went about all of the differences. The much shorter and to the point version was aged beef is tastier and far more tender. As I listened (as intently as I could) so that I could design a cooler that would handle his needs, I was thinking why doesn't he just shut up. I also began to think..." why can't I do the same thing with my venison?" Suddenly instead of thinking "hurry up and finish so I can design your box" ...I began to ask him questions. His face lit up like a Christmas tree. He had probably been talking his poor wife's ear off about this same topic for years without her ever asking him anything other than to "change the subject!" There were, according to him several ways to keep his product from drying out while ageing it. The two which interested me the most were keeping the meat covered as it aged and keeping the proper amount of air flow over the meat. I designed him what he later deemed as the perfect cooler, and he taught me the **Perfect Way** to prepare venison... by first ageing the meat either before you process it or before you take it to your favorite local processor.

After I finished with my sales meeting, I went straight out to the farm, well almost. I stopped along the way and bought some plastic to cover my buck in. When I got to the farm, I first covered the meat in the way my customer/mentor had described, and then I made some adjustments to the cooler itself to achieve the proper air flow and temperature. I allowed that deer to hang in the cooler for two more weeks before I cut it up and processed it. The end result was simply delicious. It was a totally different piece of meat all together. Before I might have taken the hind quarters off the deer and ground them up into hamburger, I now carved them into roasts. I put the first of these on my spit at home and slowly smoked it as it turned. The result was a wonderful venison creation which was juicy and so tender that could be cut with a fork! My family has been hooked ever since. When I first started hunting, they would unenthusiastically eat the meat that I brought home. My predecessor had also been a hunter. It turns out he was a great guy, but perhaps not the best venison chef on the planet. They would eat what I served because they knew me to be a creative cook. Now they anxiously awaited my bringing home more meat. "I got a deer" took on a whole new meaning for my family.

By hanging an animal in the cooler, I could control the amount of gaminess in the meat by how long I allowed it to hang. By allowing the enzymes in the meat to break it down into a more tender state I was creating a whole new and improved venison. ***Instead of covering the carcass in plastic, simply leave the hide on the meat***. It's the perfect cover. The hide allows the meat to breath, without allowing an excessive amount of air to flow over the meat... Sorry I'm getting as carried away with this as my customer did before I made the transition. You readers may be thinking "why doesn't he just shut up?" This is supposed to be a book on learning to hunt! On and on I went with this dissertation when perhaps all **you** wanted to ask me was to "change the subject!" The much shorter and to the point version is that aged venison is much tastier, and far more tender!

Always look for and exchange with other hunters, cooks and chefs' different ways to prepare your wild game. **And always allow it to age in some sort of a hanging cooler! You'll never go back to the old way.**

Another way to ensure top quality meat is to drop the animal in question in its tracks. It's the exact opposite of a herd of cattle awaiting their turn at the slaughterhouse. One minute the animal you're hunting is standing there minding its own...and the next it's down. No fear, no running, no adrenalin and no cortisol. *It is also the humane way to acquire meat. The animal doesn't suffer the anguish of knowing what's about to happen. Cut the animal when you recover it to get the blood out and either field dress it right there or as quickly as possible get it back to the skinning rack and get the heat out of the carcass as soon as you can.*

Triangle Double Ladder

The stand that Joe and Vernon were checking out on the day that we "invented" the Koala Stand was a replacement for the low boy in the triangle. The pine trees had grown up to where they were taller than the low boy thus rendering it practically useless. Its replacement was a new double ladder stand. Rather than being in the center of the triangle like the low boy had been, this stand was located on the lower side of the field near the creek bottom. It looked into the thickness of the triangle as well as up on top of the field where a stand of oaks was located. Off to the left was the thick and nasty bedding area where the disappearing six pointer had come from on that fateful day. They had chosen well as usual. Our rule at the farm was if you shot a buck, you could not pull the trigger on your second buck for that season until you took a doe. This was done to help keep the doe to buck ratio in balance. I was searching for my doe, and this was as good a place as any to begin my quest. I settled in for a morning hunt. The stand had some issues; the morning sun which had been at your back in the low boy was now off to the right side and semi in your face. That was the morning that I learned about wearing hats when you hunt! Anything that was moving to the right of center had you looking somewhere between partially and totally into the morning sun. Without a hat, there was no way that you could look through your scope in those directions. Well, you could if you used one of your hands to cover the scope, but that left you firing a high-powered rifle with only one hand...I believe we've already covered that subject in another chapter!!! I had been known to do some stupid things while learning to hunt but I'm not "generally" stupid enough to make the same mistake twice. I especially wasn't going to make it from twenty feet up in a tree. As luck would have it, a very large buck happened to be on the morning blind side of the field that morning. Not that I could have done anything about it anyway, I hadn't killed my mandatory doe yet. I resolved myself to watching the beautiful animal through my binoculars. It wasn't a particularly easy part of the field to hunt anyway. We had cut a path through the young pines with the brush hog which criss-crossed the field. Anything that wasn't on that path was close to impossible to see and was thus unfair to shoot at. I enjoyed part of the morning watching the buck work his way through the field while scent checking for does. He came into view only to disappear. Then he would reappear and then vanish yet again. I finally heard movement in the thick trees to my left. I slowly moved my attention span away from the buck in the sun and began to focus on whatever was on my left side. Maybe five min-utes later, the "mover appeared in the path. It was the doe that I'd been looking for. I patiently waited for her to work her way into a good firing solution for me. I wasn't going to risk a bad shot on her and so far, that was all she had offered. Eventually the trail she was on would turn up towards the oaks and that would offer me a broadside shot (providing of course that she stayed on the path). She did stay on it, when she got to the spot where I wanted her to be, I whistled to stop her. When she hit the brakes, I squeezed the trigger. She never knew what happened. That's the ultimate way to put an animal on the ground. No suffering or anguish was involved at all. As I watched her from my stand even though I was sure that she was dead, I began to ponder about the big buck. Was he now legal by club rules? Was it wrong to shoot him when I already had an animal on the ground? Had he bolted at the sound of my rifle shot? The only question that I could answer for sure was whether he was still in the area and even that was not going to be for sure unless I saw him. As it turns out, I never did see him again that day or any other that season, but he'd be back. We watched him for two more seasons and never did get a shot on him. He became the bruiser of the forest. And you know what... "That's Hunting!"

After ample wait on both the doe on the ground and on whether to big buck was still in the area, I unloaded my rifle, packed up my gear and lowered it to the ground. I reloaded my gun and went to check on the doe. She was down for good. I walked back to the cabin and got the four-wheeler. Then I came back, loaded her up and took her back to camp to clean her up for the cooler. It took considerably less time to get her ready for hanging since I didn't have to skin her. That was a plus for the new way of processing! I called Vernon and put the questions of the morning to him. It turns out that there was no problem with shooting two deer in the same day or even in the same hunt. Both were legal in South Carolina and both were accepted at Balenacre. Question two was a little bit trickier. "Technically I guess someone would have to witness which order they were shot in" said Bwana. "But there would be no doubt in my mind that if you told me which order you shot in, I'd believe you." That was an unnecessary affirmation on his part, but it still felt nice to know that he knew we had the same moral convection on both the rules and the truth. The whole time we hunted his property together and for our ongoing friend-ship since for that matter, I've done everything within my power to never betray that mutual trust I had with my friend.

Club rules are meant to be followed. They aren't something that you follow on some whim or that you can say well I agree with this rule so I'll follow it but I don't like that rule so I'll bend it to suit my needs. Our rule of a doe following a buck was set before I ever got there. Plus, I happened to agree with the reasoning behind the rule. Even if I didn't, I would still follow the rule. Did it cause me to miss the opportunity to take that magnificent animal? Not the way I see it. First and fore-most, I had just taken a very nice sized buck even if his rack wasn't perfect. Second, I'll use the analogy of the hunting sanctuary from the earlier story. If you chase all the deer off of the property then what are you going to hunt?) Paraphrase that just a little and you might have a statement that went something like this..." if I wasn't willing to follow the club's rules then I wouldn't have been there to miss the chance to shoot that buck anyway!" And finally, I've already stated and shown through my actions multiple times that I'm unwilling to take a bad shot on an animal buck or doe and risk wounding it. That buck was directly in the morning sun, and I wasn't wearing a hat. I would have been squinting through my scope under the best conditions. I would not have taken that shot. You don't have rules for that situation...just a conscience.

*Likewise, I could have taken five or six bad angle shots at the doe that was walking towards me that morning. Any one of them might have killed her but then again, they might have not. I waited until I knew I could make a clean and swift kill shot before I tickled the trigger. **Only shoot when you know you can effectively kill.***

We used four wheelers at Balenacre. We used them a lot in fact, but we did not use them as a means of transportation to and from stand sites. We walked! You can quietly get in and quietly get out without education the deer to our presence. You can use that walk to enjoy nature...which should be why you're in the woods in the first place. You can use the walk in or the walk out to scout for signs. Or you can still hunt into your stand and then still hunt back to camp thus prolonging your hunting time and improving both your skills as a hunter and your chances of taking an animal. **Every story you'll hear about Balenacre that ends in a successful kill will ultimately have the phrase "I then walked back to camp and got the four-wheeler to retrieve my deer" in it.**

Friends are one of the only things you get to choose in life! Trust between friends is irreversible once it's lost. If I can't trust my wife or my best friend or worse, if either one of them loose faith in me...Go ahead and put me in the grave!

Guests

Joe once made a comment when Vern asked what he thought we should do about hunting guest..." Shoot em!" He was kidding of course... well mostly anyway. What he was trying to say in his eloquent way was members put in all of the funds and the effort that make a club work in the first place. Then we start bringing in two or three guest every weekend and ultimately you'll end up with a club that has thirty full time members with only six of them paying for upkeep and doing the work so all the rest can enjoy our efforts for free. That's what happens if there aren't certain rules regarding guests.

The other side of that coin is (and Joe fully agrees with me) that we want to share our life-style with other people. We especially want to share it with people who don't or haven't yet experienced it. So, we have rules to keep the sharing of that experience within reason. They work and they should be followed by everyone.

The afternoon after I had shot the doe in the triangle my buddy Jey showed up with a friend of his and his two young sons. If I remember correctly the older boy played little league ball with Jey's son Gains. He introduced me to them. Like Jey and Gains, they were delightful people. The boys all took to being boys in the front yard while the adults (and I) talked. This was what I had missed out on as a kid with my dad and the thought was not lost on me. After a little boyish roughhousing, their fathers called them inside to clean up to go hunting. They chose stands which would house their sons and off they went for their afternoon hunts. I chose my stand and went off as well. The big entertainment for the evening was not who shot what, but rather the boy's exuberance over having gone hunting at all. Again, this was the type of thing that I hadn't enjoyed as a kid, and I loved every minute of their reactions over what they had seen. They were recalling the different animals in the woods, the sounds; they even did a pretty good job of describing their own excitement over the whole hunting experience. After dinner we watched a little football on the tube until it was bedtime for the kids. Their dads put them down which was no easy task. I may not have gone hunting with my dad, but we did plenty of camping and I'm sure he had the same issues quieting excited young boys before lights out. Once they were down, the dads shared their versions of the hunts with me. There was lots of emphasis on squirming and noise. The two older kids stayed pretty interested in what was happening, but the little guy had his moments. The biggest problem was having an eight-year-old and a six-year-old in the same stand with an adult. That had to be cramped. As the evening went on, Jey's friend seemed to understand that I had a way with kids. Once I was sure that he felt comfortable enough, I offered to solve his problem. "If you're OK with the idea, I'll take one of your boys with me in the morning. That way you won't be so cramped up. That will make all the difference in the world to the little guy." I could tell that he loved the idea. He said "I wouldn't want to ruin your hunt" I assured him that I would much rather take one of his kids out in the morning and see absolutely nothing than shoot the buck of my dreams. "Why" he asked. "So I could see for myself what my father had missed out on when I was their age" I answered. That hit home. "If you're sure you don't mind, that would be great" he said. "I don't mind a bit, which kid do you want me to take?" "Well, again if you don't mind, I'd kind of like for my eight-year-old to take his first shot at a deer" he said. "I'm sure that you'd like to be there for that, why don't you let me take the little guy with me then" I asked. "Well, you're right" he said, "I would love to have that moment with my boy, but I'm pretty sure the little one will wreck your hunt." "I doubt it" I countered "I'll love every squirming minute of it!" With that exchange it was settled.

The next morning the boys were told of our new arrangement. They took it all in stride as they ate their cereal. I took the young-n to the box stand in the long field. He promised his daddy "I'll be good" and they said their good-byes. I helped him into the stand and set up the extra folding chair that I had brought along for him. He played "20 questions (or maybe 21 or 22) with me. "Mr. Mark, what's that" he asked about my range finder. I told him what it was and how it worked. "Can I try it" was the next question. "Of course you can" I said. "I'll share everything with you except my riffle." "That's OK" he whispered, "my daddy won't allow me to shoot yet anyway." He played with the range finder for a while and then asked, "Mr. Mark can I look through your pack?" "Sure you can" I said "but do it quietly." He very meticulously pulled out one thing at a time and asked what each one was in a quiet voice. I satisfied his curiosity just as quietly about each item. He finally got down to my calls. "What's that Mr. Mark" he asked once again. "That's a grunt tube" I answered him. "What do you do with it" he asked. "You call Mr. Deer with it. His eyes were as big as saucers. "Do they answer you" he questioned. "Sometimes" I answered him. "Wow" he said. "And what's that Mr. Mark" he asked about my doe in heat can." Once again I answered him "we use that to talk to Mrs. Deer." "Does she answer too" he asked in a little bit less of a whisper. "Sometimes she does" I said. "Wow" he said again..." can I try" he asked. "Of course you can, I said I would share everything but my riffle" I answered him. I showed him how each of the calls worked. He was amazed. I devised a game that kept him entertained for the rest of the morning. "OK every twenty minutes you can alternate between the doe call and the buck call." He spent almost as much time looking at his watch to see if it was time to call Mr. Buck or Mrs. Doe as he did watching the field. He did spend a fair amount of time watching animals through my binoculars though. We never saw any deer that morning, but we saw lots of other wildlife and the two kids (one big and one small) had a blast. When his dad came by to pick us up, he was surprised to find that his young son wanted to hunt some more. "You're not sleepy or bored" his dad asked. "No sir" he answered politely, "we've been talking to Mr. Buck and Mrs. Doe all morning. They haven't answered me back yet but I'm sure that they're about to any minute. Can we stay and try for a little bit longer daddy, PLEASE!" "Sure we can son, if you really want to." We switched places and I explained the game to his dad. "You can change the rules to whatever you like" I said. "If it ain't broke, don't fix it" was his seal of approval! **WITH THAT, I ENDED ONE OF THE VERY BEST HUNTS I'VE EVER BEEN ON.**

If you ever get the chance to take a kid hunting for the first time...DO IT! I'll wager you won't see very many deer if you see any at all, but I'll also bet that when you're done you'll feel the same way I did.

If you find yourself with a young hunter in your stand, find a way to interact with them that actually relates to hunting. Like my hunt, it probably won't be successful in so much as harvesting any animals, but it can be extremely important to the youngster. If they can have a good time doing something related *to the art of hunting then they will stay inter-ested in it long enough to become hooked. I was just lucky and stumbled into the game with the calls but keeping him participating in the activity of hunting made all of the differ-ence in the world.*

Take a kid hunting! Do it right and you'll both be glad you did.

Hang Time

Now previously, hang time to me used to refer to how long a kick was in the air in a football game. It was always a cool thing because while the receiver is waiting for the ball with his head up watching it... some guy is running down the field like an angry bull with his eyes on nothing but the receiver. It's like watching a train wreck, you just know there's gonna be a major collision at the end! From this point in time on for me hang time has also become an art form. Hang your game too long and you end up having to cut away too much of the meat. If you don't hang it long enough, then the meat isn't as tender and can sometimes still be a bit gamy.

I let the big buck hang in the cooler for three weeks. The doe was right beside him and coming along just fine with her hide still on her. I took the buck out of the cooler and cut up the meat. At this point in time I was still using paper to wrap before freezing. I wrapped all the meat up except a roast that I had cut out of one of the hind quarters. Before hanging, I always used the quarters for burger or jerky. I took the roast (and the rest of the meat) home. The roast I put in a great marinade and allowed it to sit for the evening and most of the next day. (If you're interested, you can see the recipes section in the end of this book for the marinade as well as other tasty ways to prepare your game). The rest of the meat went in the ice box. For cooking I put the roast over a charcoal spit and turned it while I smoked it with hickory chips real slow. To give you an idea of how it tasted... it was about a five-pound roast all clean meat, no fat or bone and there were six of us eating that evening...we polished it off. All of it! So much for the old half a pound of meat per person being served rule. I knew that I was on to something really good! I made a commitment to myself after that meal to make sure to harvest one more deer before the season was over. Otherwise, I was sure that I was going to run out of venison before the next season started. My family was now hooked, and I was sure that once my friends caught on, they were going to be as well. I was creating a monster and it felt great!

I was fortunate enough to get one nicer sized doe that season. It was about a week before Christmas. With my new lesson learned, I hung her in the cooler. She was to hang with her hide on for three weeks before I would go about the chore of processing her meat. I felt like three good sized deer would be enough meat to last me my family and some of my friends for the next year. With that done, I rushed off to do some last-minute Christmas shopping for my wife. Actually, it wasn't last minute at all. I had found a beautiful antique door for the entry way into our house. I had to go into a little town called Waxhaw to pick it up so that I could make the adjustments needed so that it would fit in its new home.

I had received some nice Christmas gifts that were hunting oriented and couldn't wait until the next season to try them out. New Year's Day is the last day of hunting season in South Carolina. I opted to forgo the fireworks and parties to go hunting. My wife isn't big on either one. She usually ends up in bed by ten so I wouldn't be cheating her out of anything by going out to the farm. I hunted that morning and most of the day. I was seeing deer, but I opted not to shoot since I had acquired my allotment of meat for the year. There was an opportunity to take a fairly nice shooter buck later on in the hunt but again I had enough meat and just let him go. He would be a better animal next season or perhaps even two seasons later. By then he'd be something. I had guests coming out for New Year' Day dinner and so I cut my hunt short to go home and help my wife. In my haste to get back to help, I had already prepped the cabin for departure the night before. The next morning, I grabbed my gear and hit the woods. As a result, there was no need for me to go back inside when my hunt was over. I had deviated ever so slightly from my normal end of hunt routine. I just emptied the chamber in my riffle, threw it in the back and rushed home to my wife's aid. Dinner was great and it was a no harm no foul ending to the season.

Too Close For Comfort

My stepson David announced to me one afternoon that he had purchased a shotgun for home protection. He hadn't had much experience with firearms, and he asked me if I would show him how to break it down and clean it. I answered, "better than that, I haven't cleaned my gun from last season so we can do them both together." He said that would work and we set a date to do just that. When that day came David brought over his new shotgun and I drew into my arsenal and pulled out the rifle that I had used for most of the previous season; my 30.6. I remember it like it was yesterday, Dianne was in the office and David was in the kitchen. I was by our bedroom door and in front of the front door to the house. I dutifully worked the bolt action to my "empty" rifle just to make sure that it was unloaded before we began the cleaning process. Then casually like it was second nature

I aimed the gun away from anyone else just to be safe. The gun was aimed towards the front door when I pulled the trigger to dry fire it. That was undoubtedly the loudest dry firing I have ever heard. The sound of the report in our house rivaled that of the one when I fired the shotgun in the old van trailer when I first started hunting. The whole house smelled like cordite when I heard my wife's frantic question "is everyone Ok?" Still stunned I answered "yes honey we're both fine" "Dude what just happened" I remembered hearing David ask... The whole New Year's Day came rushing out from the depths of my memory banks. I had not unloaded the gun like I always do after the hunt; I had opted for the quick out of emptying the chamber and leaving the rest of the ammo in the clip and *carelessly* threw a partially unloaded gun in the back of my truck and I rushed home to help my wife prepare for our guests. I left my gear in the truck and went inside to help her. The next day I pulled it out of the truck in a rush to get to work and didn't check out my weapon before I stuffed it in the guest bedroom. Lastly it was the following weekend before I found the time to finally put away all my hunting gear for the season. Each single small seemingly harmless event had led me to ever so slightly change my meticulously rigid firearms handling routine. Since I had always followed the exact same routine, I was absolutely sure that that weapon was unloaded. IT WASN'T! That thought took only a microsecond to process... "I screwed up!" was my answer to David's question. The only thing that went right out of the whole situation and the only thing that saved the day from utter disaster was the (learned) second natured treating of a firearm...every firearm real, BB or toy, as though it is always loaded. Since it was "fictitiously" loaded, I had aimed it away from anyone in the area...unfortunately I had aimed it at my wife's antique door Christmas present which to this day still bears the scar of a hunter who became too preoccupied with making up for the fact that he was hunting when he should have stayed home and helped his mate prepare for their guests.

David took his shotgun back to the sporting goods store that same day and to my knowledge, he has never owned a gun since. That was truly a missed opportunity for us to have a common bond that could have lasted for the rest of our lives, and I very deeply regret it.

Routines are a wonderful practice when handling firearms. To do the same thing every time until it becomes second nature should be a good thing as well as common practice. In this particular instance it was both a good thing as well as a bad one. **It was bad because I deviated from my normal practice of always unloading my riffle completely after my hunt.** *In this instance, I was running late and chose erroneously to wait and unload it when I got home. To further complicate matters, I had also taken the round out of the chamber. Now in no way am I abdicating leaving a round in a chamber of a gun that you're about to transport. But at least when I went to clear the chamber at my house that fateful day, I would have sent the bullet flying through the air and thus been warned. Because I was so regimented at unloading my weapon after each hunt, I was sure that it was unloaded. The time which lapsed between the hunt and when I unloaded my gear out of the truck further complicated matters because the fact that I hadn't unloaded was no longer fresh in my memory.*

Never deviate from your routine for the safe handling of your firearms!

When you check a gun to make sure it's unloaded, don't just run the bolt in and out,

always look at the clip to make sure that there is not any ammo within.

Always treat a firearm as though it's loaded. Even if you are sure that it is not. And never ever point a weapon in the direction of another person. These last points are the only difference between an embarrassing incident and a disaster which could easily have cost someone their life.

<u>HASTE!</u> *Haste creates mistakes. That is exactly what happened to me. When you are planning a hunt, always make sure that any commitments that you may have are already taken care of. How can you enjoy a lengthy sit in nature if you are feeling guilty about something that you were supposed to be doing? If you don't have enough time to go hunting because of something else that you must do afterwards, then you are running the risk of being tempted to take shortcuts to make it to the next event. That's what happened to me. I was feeling guilty about not being at the house to help my wife with a dinner event that I had planned. I rushed to get home to her and help, and I cut some basic but dangerous corners.* **God was with me the day that I was humbled about my "expertise" with weapons and no one was hurt!** I eventually got over my embarrassment over the mishap with the door and once again began thinking about the upcoming hunting season.

The Hookie Bow

Whenever you think about the season to come, invariably you also think of the previous season's achievements as well as its shortcomings. One such shortcoming (other than killing an antique door out of season) was several missed opportunities with my bow. While I'm a deadly shot at a target, I had several opportunities to take nice deer with my big Pearson. Big was the number one problem but there were other problems as well. Its heavy draw weight made it very hard to pull down on a deer with any amount of stealth. Not being able to draw without drawing attention to myself as well had cost me a beautiful buck that season and I was now sure that it was time to put away my stubborn pride and finally purchase a modern compound bow. I went back to my friends at Nichol's Store and looked through their selection. The ultimate choice came down to a matter of cost.

They had a great sale on Alpine Bows at the time. They were just as fast as the big guys and the one I chose was almost half the size of my old bow. I purchased duplicates for all the accessories that I had ultimately gotten for the Pearson. I figured that they had served me well so far and I was used to them so the only change would be the bow itself. It was a good call. I was knocking the back out of my target in no time at all. I now had a bow that I could use in smaller places and between limbs in trees. One that I wouldn't have to grunt myself every time I strained to pull it back. I also had a backup bow. If something ever went wrong with the new bow, I could use the old Pearson while it was being repaired. I practiced with the new Alpine until I was totally confident with it. Then and only then was I ready to make the switch as far as hunting season went. Bow season came and went without me even getting in a tree. I was on a diving job in Florida for the month in which it started. By the time I returned it was gun season. No matter to me, I had a new bow and that was what I wanted to hunt with and that was what I was going to hunt with. I had never hunted bow this far into the season except for the first season I ever hunted. Like the first season I didn't get too many chances to have deer close enough to take a shot. What I hadn't counted on was that by the time gun season opened up, the deer were beginning to get spooked. In the early months of bow season, they were still in there typical bedding to feeding patterns and they were both relatively easy to pattern as well as relatively easy to sneak up on. Not so at all once the guns started booming at them. The odds were against me, and I still didn't know enough about hunting to counter those odds in my favor. Still, there I was hunting away with my new bow. I began to really see the difference between hunting with a high-powered rifle and with a bow. With a rifle, all you really have to do is be in the right place and be still. Hunting with a bow you quite literally have to draw the animals to within at least thirty yards of you without them knowing you were there. That's only the start of the complications. Next you must avoid the eyes and ears of the animals, having several in the vicinity compounds the chances of getting busted even more. Then you must learn when to try and stand, draw and aim without the deer seeing or sometimes even sensing your movement. Bow hunting in the midst of the riffle season was and still is a completely different ball game. Once you have

finally mastered all the aforementioned problems...the easy ones, that's right the easy ones
then you have to begin to learn to master the
truly hard dilemma. That would be your own
emotions. When you're bow hunting, every
single hunt where you encounter animals
is like the hunt in the "tree killer" story earlier in this book. They are right there with you
breathing the same air as you are and seeing
and hearing the same sights and sounds as
you are. The adrenalin levels go through the roof.
That is one of the most exciting things about
bow hunting. It is also one of the most difficult
challenges to overcome. If you can't control
your excitement, then you can't make a good
clean shot. I fell in love with bow hunting that
season. For the most part, I was busted in one
way or another on most of the hunts where I
saw animals. That didn't seem to matter to me
one bit. Just being in the same location with
them was enough to keep me coming back for
more again and again. Just like when I was
first learning to hunt, every single time I was
busted was a lesson learned. Many of those
lessons also came with a good laugh as well
but they were still lessons.

One such lesson came and shortly afterwards I designated my old Pearson as the

Hooky bow. I took the old bow out to my warehouse one morning just to have it so I could launch some arrows at my "block" target. No, I wasn't regressing backwards to my old days of shooting paper plates...it actually is called "the block." I never got the chance to take any target practice that day because I got very busy. By the time the rush was over it was about the time I would be getting ready to go in the woods if it were a day that I had been planning on hunting. "Why not" I thought? "I'm here and I have my bow. I'll just clean up change cloths and climb up in my old tree fort. I hunted that evening but didn't see anything. I got down changed back into my work cloths and drove home. When I came through the front door, my sweet wife had dinner all ready for her "hard working husband!" To her, I had just turned in a long day at the office. It took a little bit of time for that to sink in and I just let it ride. All my hunting gear was at the house. My guns, my hunting bow my camo...so by her way of thinking I had just been working late. It wasn't visions of sugar plums that were dancing through my head at that moment... it was more like wow, that's like a permanent kitchen pass any time I want one! At least once a week from that point on I had to work late. After daylight savings time was over it really wasn't that much time, it was just an extra hour or two of bow hunting that I didn't have to answer about. I just left the Hooky Bow at the warehouse with some extra camo and would hunt my place in the afternoon after my work was done. I never lied about whether I had been hunting on those days. I never had to; it was just assumed that if all my gear was at the house, I was working. Had Dianne ever asked, I would have of course told her the truth. She just never did. It was kind of like the military's policy of don't ask don't tell...it didn't come up, so it didn't matter. We men are never as smart as we sometimes think we are. I found out years later that Dianne had caught on to my "hooky bow" action within a month of its inception. She was just too sweet to break my heart by bringing it up. It was "don't ask don't tell in reverse. It was like being a little boy again. I had my secret fort that "only I knew about "that I could go and hide in any time I needed to get away from it all. Trouble was, in reality, my father knew where my fort was. Most of my friends knew and if they had ever been pressed they would have squealed on me like a stuck pig. The only exception would have been my father. He would have never "ratted" me out. My fort was only special because it was "secret". It was only secret because I wanted to believe that it was! My hooky bow was only a secret because my wife (like my father) wanted me to believe that it was a secret! What a wonderful woman I married!

I spent years hunting with the hooky bow on that one day a week basis. I had several close encounters but none of them ended with me putting meat on the table. That big giant of a bow was just too much to hide with. Of course, I was still the only person that I knew who could draw it back but what did that matter if every time that I pulled it on a deer I roared like a weightlifter. It's kind of hard to surprise an animal as well suited for the woods as a white-tail deer is with that kind of approach.

Waiting For The Bus

I had learned on my property getting ultra clean had an adverse effect on the deer population. It seemed that they were used to the farmers in the field all sweaty and sometimes greasy and grimy. Now those farmers never attacked the deer or tried to harm them in any way. By my way of thinking, the deer learned to associate the smelly humans as non-threatening to them. So, by going into the stand straight from work "al natural" so to speak, I was as close to invisible to the deer as I could get. One particular afternoon I had been in the stand for about twenty minutes when a couple of does came to the edge of the dry creek bed which is in the middle of that funnel of woods where I hunted. They were about forty yards away from me. That is a makeable though not advisable shot with a modern compound bow. Or course we've already established that the Hooky was not a modern bow. I wasn't hunting does anyway. I watched them for around ten minutes or so. One at a time they would nervously look back into the woods off to my left like they were waiting for the bus or something. Sure enough, the bus came out to "pick them up". The bus turned out to be a big nine pointer. This was a perfect setup. The does were to my right at the edge of the draw while the buck was to the left placing me right in the middle. If the buck went to the does he would have to cross right in front of me. As he began to "move through the crowded bar to ask them to dance" I tried to draw back the big Pearson. The does had been paying nervous attention to their would-be suitor but one of them noticed my movement. I froze at mid draw which is no easy feat with a draw weight of 100 pounds. It was almost a minute that I was stuck in that predicament. Eventually the doe lost interest in whatever might have been in the trees and once again was watching her "new companion". I was able to relax my draw and get the feeling back into my arms while they lovingly "stared across the room at one another." After another minute of this, the big guy started towards the two ladies of the night again. I tried to draw once again, this time the other doe sensed that something wasn't right.

Like her travel mate, she caught me in mid draw. I had to gut it out again. This time when the doe refocused on the moving buck I took the opportunity to come to full draw instead of relaxing. The buck "only had eyes for them" as the song goes, but the does still weren't happy about whatever had spooked them. Their demeanor was spreading to the buck who was slowly moving towards them and straight towards my open shooting lane. Just a few more steps and he'd be broadside to me at twenty yards. A shot I could make in my sleep. In fact, I had done so many times already...In my sleep! Out of the corner of my eye I could sense more than see that the does were ready to bolt. One of them was stomping the ground with her front hoof. The buck was still heading towards the antsy deer. My attention span was now split between my throbbing arms, the two does and the approaching buck. One of the does, I don't know which one, blew and they both ran off. The heartbroken buck began to trot after them right into my shooting lane. I let loose cupids' arrow and was rewarded with a solid sounding smack! I'd done it! I connected on a big buck with my Hooky bow! My whole body was shaking, not just my arms. I dutifully calmed myself and went about the painful task of sitting still for the next half hour. As I did, the entire hunt seemed to play itself once again in my mind. Everything was just like a script from a hunting show. The does to my right, and the buck to my left walking towards the shooting lane. The only things missing were dramatic music, the narrator whispering "he's a shooter," and my wife asking "didn't we just watch this last week" ...? The moment of impact was a bit fuzzy, but I had heard the smack. I was sure he was hit. I concentrated of where the animal had been when I released the arrow. Next, I found some landmarks where I had last seen the buck running off. I was already working on my blood trail. Finally, it was time to go after my buck. I was so excited as I lowered my gear from the stand and climbed down. I covered the ground to the point of impact in about five steps only to stop dead in my tracks right in front of the spot where my first hooky bow kill was to have happened. It seemed that my arrow had been suspended in mid-flight! It was just floating in midair right before the point of impact. This was as confusing as the disappearing deer had been. How could the arrow have just stopped? Robin Hood couldn't have done what I had just done...well maybe he could have but why would he have wanted to? I had split a small branch which was barely even noticeable at this distance let alone twenty yards away and up in a tree. The arrow had been on its way to history...speeding right towards the beautiful buck's vitals to put him down with a clean kill. A damned twig! Not even a full-fledged branch. How in the heck I managed to split it into and stop my arrow in mid-flight I'll never know but there it was...like a bullet from one of Neo's guns, just hovering... stopped short of its glory by some wood.

I still own my Hooky Bow. It is kept in shooting shape and hangs on the wall in my office. I still practice with it on a regular basis. I enjoy shooting it more than any other bow I've ever owned. From time to time I still take it into the woods to try and claim the victory that has eluded me for so long. It was my first hunting weapon. I learned to shoot with it. I took many a razzing over its very existence let alone that I was trying to hunt whitetails with it. One day it will happen and when it finally does, that will be the sweetest meat ever to touch my plate. Call it stupid, call it stubbornness or call it destiny but we hunters are patient if we aren't anything else.

Scraping Up A Storm

There are three main reasons why I hunt. The love of nature is the first. The thrill of the fair chase in the hunt would be the second... the third (and the most valued) is meat. I love the feeling of gathering food with my own hands for my existence. My new-found total passion for bow hunting was going beyond my love of being in nature and truly beginning to satisfy my sense of "fair chase", but it was going to become a problem as far as harvesting food for the table. As the season was coming to a close, I made the choice to switch back to my rifle and "go shopping".

What a difference a decision can sometimes make. The rut was now over, and I hadn't taken any deer. I had seen plenty and had enjoyed some very good hunting but had ultimately run scared and placed the bow on a back burner in order to obtain meat. It wasn't as if I didn't know where to find the deer, I just wasn't able to get them within range of my bow very often, and that was not a problem with my rifle. Two days later I had a 120-pound doe hanging in the cooler. The next weekend I had another. So, with the fear of eating tags officially over. One more would do me for the year and I thought it may as well be the big boy on the property. I knew where his general hangout was, and I knew where his main scrape was. The trouble was that he had gone almost completely nocturnal. Ok this is a dilemma which has haunted hunters since Troglodytes started tumbling rocks down on their prey... how do you make a nocturnal buck want to come out during daylight hours? The answer is simpler than you might think. The truth is you don't! You cannot make a whitetail deer want to come out during daylight hours once they have decided to go nocturnal. They must want to do so on their own. Ok, new question... What will make a cagey old buck want to come out of his evening hiding place in broad daylight? Three things will make a buck WANT to venture out in broad daylight. The first is LOVE! Alright maybe not love, but the desire to breed. The rut has consistently been making fools out of the wisest of animals in the wild for eons. They want to breed, so they're willing to give up the cover of darkness in order to find hot does.

Great but the first rut was over, and the second hadn't begun yet. The first option wasn't going to help me with my dilemma. The next reason an animal will want to venture out during daylight hours is food. In extreme cold environments, a whitetail deer must eat every four to six hours. If you know where their bedding and where a good food source is, and you happen to be a good enough hunter to do so, then you can set up an ambush in between the two areas and possible have a shot opportunity. Well, I was certainly trying, but I hadn't reached that level of hunting at this point in my life. To set up a stand site in Mr. Big's back yard without him knowing about it takes skills which at that point I did not possess yet.

An article in North American Whitetail Magazine entitled "Scrapping Up a Storm" offered an idea which was ultimately to prove to me a third way to make a trophy buck almost be compelled to come out during daylight hours. Rainstorms. The article indicated a theory that "no self-respecting whitetail buck will allow his scent to remain washed out of his primary scrape during mating season." If a major rainstorm came along and washed his scent out of his scrape, then the second the storm ended, that buck would be driven by primal forces to go to his primary scrape to "freshen it up a bit!"

"IT'S HIM!"

This was a sound theory to my way of thinking. It was within reason in the realm of nature, and it was "out there" just enough to be worth trying at least once. I spent years racing sailboats before I learned to hunt. I know weather patterns in my area every bit as well as the weather people. I began watching for a well-formed weather front with a defined ending, one that would end during daylight hours. We hunters are nothing if we are not patient. Patiently I waited for the right front to put this theory to the test. When it finally came, it found a well-prepared predator eager to embrace its fury. The storm started the evening before I was planning to hunt. Around noon I headed out to the oak ridge where I had planned my ambush. It was the same ridge from the tree killer incident. The rain was coming down in sheets. In addition to my foul weather gear, I harnessed the power of hefty trash bags; one for my body, another over my head like a cape and a third in reserve to throw over my lap once I was in my stand. I arrived at the stand site mostly dry at a quarter to one. According to my calculations I would have about another hour or two to wait. The rains had covered my entrance and I clamored up the twenty-five-foot ladder then hauled up my gear and sat down and then covered my legs with the final trash bag. I felt impervious to the storm! It wasn't a thunderstorm, so lightning wasn't a factor. I was actually enjoying the whole scene immensely. Like a little kid in a tent! I can remember laughing out loud as the rain continued to pour over me while I remained completely dry. After an hour and a half, the rain began to lighten up right on cue. As it tapered down to a normal rain I began to shed my protective plastic outerwear while the sound of the rain would still cover the noise of its removal. Almost as I had shed the last of the trash bags the rain switched to a drizzle and shortly thereafter stopped as if someone had turned off the faucet in a shower.

I pulled my rifle out of its rainproof cover. That was another one of my inventions which failed to produce me any money. The silence after the pounding of the rain was all most eerie. I was now in "His" backyard and directly over the top of his primary scrape and he didn't even know it. The stand I was in was called the salt lick. Why you ask...do you really need to ask? It was near the top of a very steep hill which led from the creek bottom down below. Directly across from that creek was the back forty with the young pines. I was sure that this was where he was bedding. No more than ten minutes passed before I sensed movement coming up the hill from the creek bed. I readied myself and waited with my attention on the area where I sensed the movement. I was not disappointed! Before I saw anything else, I saw antlers. Big antlers and they were continuing to seemingly rise up from the hill with each step the buck took. He was coming directly up the hill. He was a buck on a mission. He was obviously on his way to the scrape to resupply it with his "cologne." This theory really was panning out! It was the middle of the day and I mean no less than ten minutes from the time the rain stopped he was on location and on his way to my little reception. His big, beautiful head was now in plain sight and the rest of him was continuing to materialize from beneath the crest of the hill. I was being rewarded for my patience with a wonderful view of his bust when I heard some idiot practically yell "IT'S HIM!" The buck lifted his magnificent head even higher and looked directly towards the sound of the intruder. No wait, he wasn't looking at the stupid intruder, he was looking directly at ME! Surely it wasn't me who uttered those ridicules words...or was it? "Oh no you didn't" I remember thinking to myself as the giant monarch almost calmly turned and started back down the hill in the direction that he had come from. "Oh no you don't" I said as he disappeared from my view. I jumped up threw my riffle over my shoulder and slid down the ladder navy style. It wasn't exactly graceful when I hit the bottom, but I managed to stay on my feet and immediately start down the hill after the buck. I went about ten yards over the crest of the hill and there he was about forty yards to my right. I slowed to stalk speed and made my way to the first tree which offered cover. I raised my scope to my eyes when he turned and calmly walked further down the hill. I continued to stalk him down the hill...another ten or so yards and there he was again. Once more I tried to line up the shot only to have him saunter off right before I could fire. This time I heard his hoofs on the flat rocks in the creek bed. "Got you" I said to myself. On the other side of the creek was a trail which led back to the left towards the bedding area. The buck was perhaps fifty yards to my right and across the creek on the trail heading back to the left towards me. I hit the creek full steam to head him off at the pass...er, ah tha creek.

There are two things you need to know about the terrain before I continue...First, the creek bed that I was now running thru was one big flat rock. It looked like a small, wet landing strip. At that spot there was maybe four inches of ice-cold water running over it. The second thing is that when I said the rock was flat, I failed to mention that there was one spot in the rock which had about a four-inch fissure. It looked as though a brick mason had come in and laid a row of bricks straight across the creek but only in that one spot.

Now remember it had been raining hard all night and for half of the day. My muck boots had a solid two inches of red clay on them when I hit that wet rock. I had made it about halfway across when all the elements of the "Perfect Storm" were finally in place...flat rock... me running full steam through four inches of water... two inches of mud on my boots... four-inch fissure... yea that about covers it! The only logical thing left for me to do was a one and a half gainer with a half twist! It's the perfect dive when hunting whitetail deer in cold water! I received scores of 9.5s from all but the Russian judge! He mumbled something about the degree of difficulty not being high enough and then complained about my landing on the fissured rock instead of the flat part. You never can trust those Russian judges to be fair!

I remember hearing a cracking sound then I was looking up at a grey sky with ice cold water flowing all around my numb body. For the second time that day I heard myself uttering profoundly true words that were utterly stupid! "HURT" was what I heard myself saying...And I of course was! Well, the hunt was over, and the deer had won. That's not unusual in hunting but the hunters generally aren't the ones who are injured at the end of the day. Not so of this day at all. I was hurt, and I knew it. After laying in the frigid water for another minute gathering my wits about me, I knew that I needed to get out of the water and get to the cabin to dry off before I became hypothermic. As I tried to stand, I realized that the cracking sound I heard when I fell was my ribs. I literally "gave up the chase" gathered up my gear which was anything but pleasant and then limped back to camp. I jumped in a hot shower and stayed there until I stopped shivering. When I got out, Earnest had arrived for the evening. He started in on me about taking long hot showers by myself until he realized that I was hurt. I told him the story and would have laughed just as hard as he had if I hadn't been so scared that my ribs would go through my lungs.

I didn't quite make it all the way through med school, but I did remember something in my studies about the medicinal qualities of single malt scotch! Ok I didn't go to medical school at all but there was some correlation in the back of my mind between drinking and college...Dutifully I opened the um medicine cabinet and found the scotch and began to self-medicate! We sat back and watched some hunting videos while I "healed myself". When I had proclaimed myself officially numb, I turned in for the night. The last thing I remembered hearing was Earnest questioning "Are you hunting in the morning?" "Are you crazy" I answered, "my ribs are broken, of course I'm not gonna hunt!" "Well, would you mind setting the alarm for me then" he asked. The alarm was right next to my bunk and Earnest always slept on the sofa in the den. I set the alarm for him and then drifted off to sleep.

I awakened the next morning to the sound of the alarm in my ears. I instinctively sprang up to shut it off and before I knew it, I was making more noise than the alarm clock! "My ribs" I howled in answer to Earnest's question about why I was making such a racket. I wasn't going to need coffee to wake up this morning, I was wide awake! As Earnest began to go through the routine of getting ready for his hunt every once in a while, he would tease me with a "you sure you aren't going hunting this morning?" Finally, I heard myself answering "why not?" It was Earnest's turn to ask, "Are you nuts, you have broken ribs"? "I know" I said "but I've been thinking about it, the white seats not very far from the cabin and it's a ladder stand and its only ten or twelve feet up in the air. I think it'll be ok!" Secretly I just wanted to shut him up. I knew I wasn't going back to sleep, and I knew that I could make it to the stand and climb the short distance to the top, and I had never seen a deer out of the white seat in all the years that I had hunted at Balenacre. I would just go out and enjoy the morning in nature before I packed up and went home. Well, I managed to get dressed and get into the stand without doing any bodily harm to myself. Given the previous day's events that was a good start! I settled into the morning's watch and just kind of put myself on cruise control watching nature wake up. From time to time in the off season I do just that, go and sit with no intention of hunting, just observing. For whatever reason, I almost always see more wildlife when I'm "just there." Anyway, there I was a peaceful observer of nature enjoying the animals big and small in their surroundings when I heard the familiar crunch of a hoofed animal over to my left. Now no one had ever seen him, or even filmed him but there has been since I came to the farm a scrape of monumental proportions in that very area every year. I very slowly and gently (for reasons other than not wanting to alert the deer) turned my body in the swivel seat to face the animal now working the scrape. It was a buck, a fairly nice one too. He certainly was not the one that everyone at the club had envisioned as the animal who was working that huge sign, but none the less he was most definitely a shooter. I tried to ignore the pain as I reached for my riffle, but it was not easy. I raised the gun to my shoulder and took aim at the deer. I just sat there with the riffle at the ready and my sights dead on the buck's vitals. Normally at this stage in a hunt I'm on auto pilot. I have learned that when it is time to take the shot, it's best if you are a well-oiled machine. In this instance, the machine appeared to be jammed for some reason. There I was with the perfect firing solution and my favorite riffle at my shoulder with the high-powered Burris scope centered on a shooter buck's vitals and the auto pilot was malfunctioning. Or was it? I had my favorite riffle...my trusted 30.6...the one with the synthetic stock, you remember the one that was too powerful for such a light stock...the one that Vernon vowed never to shoot again...the one that left a ring around my right eye, one shot one kill! But still I hadn't fired! Somewhere in the back of the "machine's" firing computer was a glitch which kept me from pulling the trigger. The glitch kept repeating "don't do it, this is going to hurt!" Wait a minute; maybe this wasn't a glitch in the computer at all. The computer was reminding me that I had broken ribs! The machine was in self-preservation mode, and I was too stupid to acknowledge it! The hunter in me was ten feet up a tree with a buck in his sights ready to fire, but my alter ego... the one who whined like a mule after I sat up in bed too fast, the one who limped to the stand and then climbed up in it one handed because it was too painful to use both hands...you know, the "sissy" side of me, couldn't bring myself to be brave... er ah, stupid enough to fire a high powered riffle while up in a tree with broken ribs. I think it was somewhere around six weeks that I debated with the hunter ego before I did the only thing that was not (PHYSICALLY) painful since falling in the creek the day before! I lowered the riffle. I quietly watched the buck work the scrape for another five minutes before he wondered off into the bedding area in behind him. I unloaded my gun, lowered it to the ground and climbed down out of the stand a good bit more gingerly than the exit out of the salt lick the day before. I limped back to the cabin and packed up my gear and gingerly loaded it in my truck. Then I went back inside and waited on Earnest to finish his hunt before leaving. I eased onto the sofa and started watching hunting videos and nursing my wounds (including my hunting ego) while I waited on Earnest. He came in about an hour later after seeing "nothing worth shooting" (which to him meant nothing at all). "What'd you see" he asked me? "Nothing at all" I answered him back.

I've often said that "one advantage I have over hunters whose fathers taught them everything they ever learned about hunting is that mine didn't!" Many longtime hunters become victims of their own knowledge. They sometimes think *"this is the way my father did it, it's how he taught me to do it, and it's how I'm gonna teach my kids to do it as well!"* That's great until it begins to get in their way of evolving. You can bet that prey will evolve and learn new ways to evade whatever is hunting them. Sometimes you just have to be willing to look at different approaches to age old problems. Since I didn't have to deal with the ego problem (at least not about this) of *"that's how I've always done it,* I read a lot and I'm willing to try different ways of doing things. The article I had read on Scraping Up a Storm in North American Whitetail Magazine was one of those different approaches. IT WORKS! I have successfully used this strategy numerous times since then. Given the right conditions, it has rarely failed me. Now I'm not saying that you should go off halfcocked and try every hair brained idea that you hear of from now on. You should use common sense. But if you do happen to hear a well-founded strategy which sounds reasonable...why not give it a try. Even if you ultimately decide not to try a particular idea, at least don't refuse to try it because you've never done it that way before, or *"that's not the way my daddy did it!"* I have learned lots of

very cool things about different ways to hunt by keeping an open mind on new things. You should too!

Hunting is a way of life which can easily get the best of your emotions. It's easy to become passionate about it. Passion can easily lead to becoming zealous about something. The next phrase of the day is "overly zealous" ...the one after that is **STUPID!** Sliding down a twenty-five-foot ladder with your hands and feet on the outside of the rungs is stupid. Running down a steep embankment after a heavy rain-storm is stupid. Running through a creek with muddy boots on is, yea you guessed it stupid! **Don't allow excitement to take total control of your actions...** Especially not when you're hunting. It can get you into a whole lot more trouble than just some broken ribs. While we're on the subject of ribs...Don't go hunting with broken ribs! Just my opinion but that's not a particularly a great idea either!

Now it is the wrong time to go giving myself praise for making a good decision, but there I was, up a tree with broken ribs, hunting deer. Not that I was expecting to actually see any deer but suddenly there one was. I shouldn't have been up there in the first place, but I was. I was able to show some of the reason that was *so lacking the day before and restrain myself from doing something painfully dangerous.*

I brushed on another subject in that last paragraph. I was not expecting to see any deer. I have been in the woods on enough occasions where I wasn't hunting or expecting to see animals and then seen them anyway to have formed an opinion on it. I believe that animals can sense when you mean them harm. There is something that your body gives off, some endorphin or smell or something animals can pick up on when you're stalking them. I don't think that it's just my bad luck when I'm in the woods with no weapon and suddenly you encounter wildlife. They can sense that you're not there to hunt them. Think I'm crazy? I've seen fish in the ocean swimming around with sharks, even turning their backs on them when they could "sense" that the shark wasn't in a feeding frenzy. They instinctively knew that they weren't its prey at that particular moment.

BIRD FEVER

What! There are other tasty animals out there that we can hunt as well? Really... Who knew?

For years I heard my fellow hunters continuously repeat "if I could only hunt one species on the planet it would be turkeys." Not me, not now, not ever! My one choice would be whitetail deer.

Fortunately, we don't have to stick with one choice. There are all kinds of interesting places to hunt with numerous animal species to choose from. I would very much like to try out as many as I possibly can before I check out. The next animal on my list was destined to be wild turkeys. I'd say (if possible) that I knew less about hunting turkey than I did about hunting deer when I first started with them.

One of my buddies invited me to hunt turkeys with him that following April. My ribs had recovered, and I was aching to get out in the woods, so I said "yes". Before the hunt, I watched a few videos and was sure that I had it all down pat and wouldn't need to admit that I didn't know what I was doing to him.

Wait a minute. Wasn't there a guy who learned his lesson about that kind of thing somewhere else in this book? Didn't that same person continuously reiterate that "if you don't know, ask someone who does?" Didn't he also say something to the effect of people would rather be the person with the answer than to be to person picking on the one who doesn't know? ...ah," I don't know what you're talking about... I never said anything like that...well, at least not about turkeys!"

I've paraphrased several times that "we hunters are not anything if we aren't patient". Well, "we men aren't anything if we aren't con-sistently stubborn... and sometimes downright stupid". Ok, I'm not sure if that is a famous quote or not but it should be. I like it... so undoubtedly, it will be repeated in this book again!

A few days before the infamous first hunt found me once again 'wondering' the hal-lowed halls of Nichols' Store trying to look like I knew what I was doing. I knew I needed a call of some sort, so I moseyed on over to the call section. At least I knew where it was located! It was where all the deer calls had always been during deer season. Only now they were turkey calls. I was off to a good start. So far, I hadn't had to ask any questions. I just kind of walked in place and observed what the hunters who looked like they knew what they were doing were picking up. It hadn't yet occurred to me that perhaps they were thinking that I knew what I was doing and were waiting for me to pick something up. (Maybe I wasn't the only one of my species out there!) Anyway, several guys had picked out a particular reed call so I thought "it must be a good one". For all I know it could have been the worst call on the market and when the first guy picked it out he started a chain reaction. The rest of "our species" jumped on the bus and went along for the ride that hopefully wouldn't end up at the bottom of a cliff. One minute the maker of that call was about to go belly up and the next...his stock was off the charts. Ok I'm getting a little ahead of myself; at the end of the day there were only three or four of us in line with the same call, hardly a rush on the market. Next, I needed ammo. Great, I knew where that section of the store was too. "This is easy" I thought to myself. Wait a minute, not everybody was hunting with the same type of weapon so waiting for someone to pick up a box of shells was not going to be the answer... or was it? Right there on the box it said "Turkey Loads" ...twelve gauge! This was like "hunting supplies for dummies." Ok, I had a "great" call, and a box of turkey loads for my shotgun. "That would be all of the turkey hunting gear that I would ever need"!!! Somewhere in the back of my mind I had to have been thinking... "Where have I heard that statement before?"

Of course, when I got out to my truck I just had to break open the new call and try it out as I drove down the road. The first sounds which came out of this call resembled a second grader trying to blow his first few notes on a trumpet. If I kept up that racket, I was gonna cause an accident! All right, now I needed to go somewhere and practice with my new turkey call. Someplace private! The warehouse was not far away, and the guys were out on a job, so I had the place to myself. Just like when I was teaching myself to bow hunt! Remember how well that turned out?

Well, I worked and practiced with my new call until I sounded like...well I'm not sure what I sounded like. With the bow, I could always honestly judge my progress. "Woops I missed", or "That was a little low", or "that was a bit left" until I was finally dead center. The only grey area involved was the outside perimeter of the target. With this call, everything was suddenly a matter of perception and there was grey area everywhere... no grey matter mind you, just area! Since there was no one else around to judge... er, ah laugh at the sounds I was making, eventually I was able to convince myself that I was getting the hang of it. Unfortunately, I'm not a turkey!

So, I go out to the farm the next day with "all the turkey hunting gear that I would ever need" and my new highly honed skill at calling birds. I meet up with my buddy and off we went. We walked maybe forty or so yards when he turns loose with one of his calls. "I thought you were supposed to be really good at this" I said, "That sounded more like a crow than a turkey!" "That's what it was supposed to sound like" he said, "Crows and turkeys are mortal enemies." It turned out to be one of many tricks he had in his bag. Once again it seemed as though my statement that "this would be all of the hunting gear I would ever need" had turned out to be a bit erroneous. We walked for a spell then he would try and make a tom gobble, then we'd walk, and he'd try again. Finally, Vernon (that's right the person I was trying to pull off this "I know what I'm doing charade" on was none other than Bwanna) the guy who taught me to hunt in the first place. Anyway, Vernon sets off this sequence of masterful calls that sounded like one hen trying to teach all the others how to seduce a tom...in French! He was clucking, and purring and cackling to beat the band! "You give it a try" he encouraged me. I mustered up my courage and went for it. I treated him and all of nature to a lone "Caaack"! I'm not even sure that I could have called it pathetic. I tried it again with much more conviction and heart! "Mark, stop it" said Vernon, "you're scarring all the birds away!" "Ya do it like this" he said as he sent out another of his "French lessons." Humbled, all I could think of to say was "oh!" We spent the whole morning trying to get the toms to gobble to no avail. To this day, years later Vernon has still not taken me with him on another turkey hunt. Any questions?

There's always someone out in the business world ready and willing to sell you great quantities of things that you don't need or that don't even work. Stay away from them. There are also a lot of places out there who hire a few pimpled faced kids to stand in the sporting goods section and help customers "pick things out". Try to avoid them too if you can. Then there are the true sportsman stores like my buddies down at Nichols Store who hire people who know how to hunt, know what products work and which ones don't and aren't so interested in making a sale. They advise you on the ones do and the ones which don't. You can go to those kinds of places for all of your hunting needs... including advice! You don't have to guess, just ask someone who knows more than you do.

"Booner Land"

Davie Crockett, Dan'll Boone, the "Derby" and of course Wild Turkey. What do all these things have in common? Real-estate! There all in Kentucky! The land of Boone and Crockett! OK, so Crockett hailed from Tennessee, I'm sure he went through Kentucky on his way to the Alamo. Speaking of Boone n Crockett, one more thing which that state is famous for is big deer! Right after the fall planting was done as the next season was about to get under way, Vern invited me to go with him to his family's farm in Hart County Kentucky. They have a place that borders Mammoth Cave National Park. And I do mean borders it! Fifty-six thousand un-huntable acres, and the next piece of land next to all of that is theirs! The season before, he had shown me pictures of the buck his brother Pat had taken. A one eighty class perfect monster! Add that to the stories that I had heard about his eighty-year-old dad Charles's hunts, his aunts, uncles and his cousins; even his eight-year-old niece had killed a Booner. I thought about for several weeks but finally decided that their family farm in Kentucky was not the kind of place that I wanted to hunt...YEA RIGHT! Before he got the invite fully out of his mouth, I was drooling all over myself!

We set the date for our hunting adventure for the first part of November. The problem with that date was that it was only September at the time. November was over two months away. Please don't get me wrong, not now not ever was I going to get bored with hunting Balenacre. However, instead of dreaming of locating a nice eight pointer who was outside the ears with a bit of mass, finding his patterns and searching out a spot to ambush him, I was wakening in the middle of the night with visions of incredibly large bruisers with mass that I couldn't get my hands around. These were the type of animals at Mammoth Cave. With headgear that made them look like they were about to topple over. All I'm saying was that it was harder than it had ever been to be totally engrossed with the upcoming season in South Carolina with Kentucky on my mind.

Finally, with some meat in the cooler hanging (which is always a plus) the weekend before the trip arrived. Now I don't want to appear overly excited or anything, but I'd already organized every bit of my hunting gear and even vacuum bagged the cloths into categories for each type of weather I might encounter. We loaded up the four-wheeler and several of our stands and some cameras for scouting. We had sleeping gear, food, beer, guns, bows and scent. We looked like a couple of kids running away from home...for good! It was time for our second problem... How were we going to fit all this stuff into one truck with a little trailer? Oh well it was a very healthy problem and we happily figured it out! Once we got the truck and trailer loaded to our satisfaction, we got a good night's sleep at our perspective houses we met at my house early the next morning and were off to Kentucky.

During the first part of the ride, Vernon slept while I drove. As I worked my way up the steep, scenic Smoky Mountains of North Carolina in silence we were passed a car. A small boy was looking out of the rear window at us in awe. At that moment it occurred to me that I had become who I had set out to be. As a young boy, riding in the cab my father's truck, I would enviously look down at the members of the "secret society" as they passed us by. In my imagination, I saw them as knights on their way to their sacred quest. Instead of carts with horses, jousting poles and armor, they would pass us in their four wheeled drive trucks with rifles in the rear windows, pulling trailers with four wheelers and climbing stands. (Not that as a boy I knew what any of that stuff was) I just saw it as part of their mysterious culture. Now I was one of their clan! I was the one in the four wheeled drive truck, with the four-wheeler and all the gear. I was on my own search for the Holy Grail. The young boy was gazing at the "boy" from the past who was now what he had dreamed of becoming. So often in life the reality of the things that we dream of as children are not as glorious as we imagined them to be. This had not proven to be the case with hunting. It was all that and so much more. There have not been many events in my life that have filled me with such gratification as I had at that moment. I have never spoken of it until now. I was truly happy deep within my soul.

Vernon woke a short time later and broke the spell of the memory from my childhood. We switched driving duties and he began to tell me about the layout of the land we were going to be hunting. He told me about important things like funnels and pinch points which had proved to be successful in years past. For sure if they had been successful in the past they would be again. With fifty-six thousand acres behind us with no hunting pressure whatsoever for sure a new deer would always be around the block to take the place of the one taken the season before. I confessed to Vern my deep-seated fear that because I was not used to deer of this caliber, I was afraid that I would take a buck that was not of the standard we were hunting. He assured me that I would not have been with him on this trip if I had not been ready to make the right call. Bwana does not give many complements and I recognized that to be one of the few. His comment just fueled the fire and deepened the satisfaction within me. That moment with the boy on the ride up to Kentucky itself would, in later reflection, prove to be the climax of the whole hunting trip. Perhaps my whole hunting career. But here I am again getting ahead of myself. After all we were on our quest to the land of giants.

We arrived at the farm as evening was about to close in on us. Although this was to be for me primarily a bow hunt, we did bring riffles with us. As such I had my trusty.06. With no time for hanging a suitable stand for bow hunting, I was encouraged by the brothers to climb up in their dad's favorite box stands with my gun. The stand was literally within sight of the family's rustic cabin. Despite all the wonderful hideouts which we had discussed over the past few months, they assured me that more quality deer had been seen as well as shot from that stand than any other on the property. I walked down to the stand hugging the tree line for cover. I also paid careful attention not to cross over any area where deer might also be using so as not to alarm them with my scent. As I settled into the stand it truly hit me where I was. My back was sixty yards away from a narrow, almost one lane gravel asphalt road. That road was all that separated the land I was hunting from the deep woods of the park. I was here, in a place where magic could happen at any time. But this wasn't any old time, it was the pre-rut! It was the time that had become my favorite for hunting. The big guys were out and searching for the first estrus does. Oh, they were most definitely still patternable. It was a time when they would move from their bedding areas to check their scrapes daily. They were looking for signs of the impending rut. All that was needed was some non-aggressive scouting to find their scrapes and then a good spot from which to ambush them. The things I had learned to do over the past few years...

MOVEMENT! In my absent-minded moment of daydreaming I had let my hunting instincts go blank. Now off to my right and coming directly from the road and thus from the park behind it was a buck! I had only been in the stand for ten minutes. I watched him emerge from the woods and into the open where he casually turned to his left. He was headed right towards my stand and would cross no more than forty yards in front of me. He was in no big hurry but still it all happened fast. He walked over to a scrape which I had not yet located in the short time that I had been daydreaming in the stand. That gave me the time I needed to count his points. He was a ten pointer. My fears were coming to pass right in front of me not only on the first day of the hunt but in the first ten minutes of it. Here was the biggest deer that I had ever encountered, but his massive body size had somehow made his rack appear small. Or did it? I couldn't tell. For the first time since the days of the "disappearing deer" I was indecisive. I sat there with the sights of my gun on his vitals and tried to decide if that was the deer I was looking for of not. The buck however was not as patient as I was and

decided not to wait on my decision. He continued off towards the left and continued to
give me a lessening target to shoot at. By the
time I decided to take him, I was unhappy with
the angle he was giving me. I lifted my gun and
let him walk out of sight never to be seen again.
I may have been in the land of opportunity, but
I was not about to take an unethical shot. That
thought pattern was exactly what had gotten
me an invitation to here in the first place. After
dusk fell, I walked back up to the cabin popped
the top and told the brothers what had happened. I took the razzing like a man, and we all
had a good laugh. The next morning after a
quick gun hunt, we put the rifles away and
began scouting for sign and a place to set up
with our bows. We found plenty of both and set
our available stands plus a couple Pat had let
us use. That evening, the brother's sister Tanna
brought their eighty something year old father
out to the farmhouse. I had met Charles years
before at Vernon's lake house. I told him of my
encounter with the ten pointer the day before.
He rewarded us all with all kinds of wonderful
memories. He was the first hunter in the state
of Kentucky to tag a whitetail deer when they
reopened deer hunting within the state. There
was an ancient black and white, faded picture

on the wall that commemorated the event. There were family moments of each of them during different stages of their lives...hunting as a family at the farm. The best, or at least my favorite story was much more recent. He told, with the help of his sons, the tale of an ancient Charles out at the property with two of his (now grown) boys. Mostly they were doing the hunting while he waited around for their success stories that weren't seeming to come in. Try as hard as they could, they weren't able to connect. The elder Charles was sitting in his cabin waiting on his sons...Vernon took over the story at that point, "There I was after another long fruitless sit, walking dejectedly back from the stand I'd been in. I was almost back to dad's field taking in the beauty of the place when the silence was broken by a resounding BAM! Evidently dad had been sitting in the cabin, walked out to the truck to get something and spotted a big buck in the field. He casually walked back to the cabin and got his rifle, then sauntered back out to the truck, leaned up against it and promptly shot the deer." Then Pat took over the story... I was coming in the other way from our aunt's property when I heard the shot. Vernon and I walked up to dad and his deer about the same time.

We'd been hunting hard for days with nothing to show for it and dad shoots a giant almost by accident. Go figure"! "All dad had to say on the subject was..." you boys go get my deer and take it out to the skinning tree and clean him up." We all had a good laugh over that one. There was a good cookin followed by more family hunting stories. Now don't get me wrong, I had a great childhood with plenty of family stories of my own, but none of them revolved around hunting roots that ran that deep. We spent the next several days hunting morning noon and night. On one of those mornings, I shot a doe. The deer in Kentucky are much bigger than they are in South Carolina. The doe probably weighed 130. I was seeing plenty of deer but not the bruiser that I was looking for. One of the evening hunts Vernon was set up on a power line clearing next to his aunt's property which had just been sold. Around dusk I heard a shot, but it sounded a little loud for Bwana's bow, so I ignored it. When I got back to the cabin Vernon was fit to be tied. It seemed that the new property owner had shot across the line and into where he was hunting. Not very safe, smart or nice so now it was Vernon's turn to be the Wookie. About that time a car pulled up in the front yard. It was a father and his little boy. They had just shot their first deer together and couldn't find it. The father said that he had heard that we were excellent hunters, and he was hoping that we would help him track his animal. He said that he wasn't positive, but he thought it was a ten pointer. That stood me up! "Where were you hunting" asked Vernon? The father answered and then Vern told him that he had shot into our property where he had been hunting. The guy apologized at least a dozen times. It was obvious that he was a rookie and didn't know any better. Vernon agreed, and we decided to go help the father son duo in locating their deer. I was very interested to see the ten-pointer. The tracking was fairly simple, and we blood trailed it for only about ten minutes before finding it. The guy could not believe it, "we must have looked for this deer for an hour and never found him" he stated. "You don't just start looking for the deer" I explained "you look for signs that it was hit and then you find its blood on the ground and follow the trail until you find the deer." "Oh" he said a little sheepishly. "You don't know what you don't know" I said back. He was once again very appreciative that we weren't harassing him and his son. Vernon held up the deer's head. It was indeed a ten pointer. "Was this the guy that you let walk the other evening" he asked me in front of the new hunter. I didn't have to look long. He was a ten pointer all right, but his Kentucky body really did make this deer's rack look small. Up close I was able to judge him to maybe be 120 inches. "No" I answered Vernon, "it's not. The one I let walk was a lot bigger than this one". He looked down at it then back up at me and said with a smirk, "you should have shot that damned deer!" "Did I do something else wrong" asked the father? "No" answered Vernon. "This was a fine deer for your first one, but for future reference, we generally let the ones this size go." The guy thanked us again and again and apologized another four or five times about the close call. "Just put it down as a lesson learned the harmless way" Vern told him and with that we parted ways. On the walk back to the cabin he asked me "How much bigger was the one that you didn't shoot Mark?" "He was probably four inches taller a good bit wider with a lot more mass" I admitted. He almost imperceptibly shook his head but to his credit he said nothing else about it the whole trip. He knew that I'd missed the deer of a lifetime and wasn't sure how I'd take it. I took it well. I was in Kentucky with my friend, and he had given me the opportunity to shoot the deer of a lifetime. It was a great hunting trip. I left Kentucky with a new outlook on hunting. I knew that I had become the hunter that I had fantasized about as a kid. We headed home in our four-wheel drive truck with the gun rack, bed full of hunting gear and a trailer with a four-wheeler on it more gear and one more thing which I did not get as a young kid...a cooler full of meat to remember the trip with.

Except for going out to the farm to process the deer that I had hanging in the cooler, I took a break from hunting for a while. I didn't hang the Kentucky doe because the meat had gotten wet in the cooler, so I spent a long afternoon processing them both and packing the meat for freezing. They would eat well. I spent some time caching up on missed work as well as some time with my wife. The rut was now in full swing in South Carolina, but I just let most of it pass. I had already hunted the rut in Kentucky and felt that was enough.

When I did get back in the saddle it was towards the end of the rut. Jey had seen a really nice eight-point buck in the area around the salt lick, but he couldn't get a fair shot at him. We put out a trail camera on a huge scrape we were certain was his. Within a few days we had pictures of HIM. That's right... it was the same deer from the year before when I broke my ribs. He was still a mainframe eight. His rack was even bigger, with more mass, but it was definitely "Him". I helped Jey in his quest to pattern the big guy. This was yet another realization that I had become the hunter that I had set out to be. Rather than having the big guy lead me through the how to's of the hunt, we were discussing strategies on the best way to close in on him and spring the trap. We came up with three good set ups in the buck's area. All of them were good and any of them would have worked but the buck had gone back to nocturnal after the main segment of the rut. The only other idea left in the bag was the same one which had gotten me injured the year before. We watched and waited for a storm that was predictable to blow in. Unfortunately, when it did, Jey couldn't make it out to the farm to intercept him at his scrape. I could though and did in fact go out on the day the front passed through. I didn't set up on the buck that Jey had been after. I felt that would be wrong even though he encouraged me to do so. There was a scrape that I knew of on my property. I took a climber in and set up on the area a few hours before the rain was to cease. This time instead of a plastic bag, I had proper rain gear. There would be no sliding down the rails of the ladder...I was in a climber. The rain began to ease and then finally ceased around 3:00. Within fifteen minutes I felt movement. That's right, if you are in tune with your surroundings, you can "feel" movement. It's more a sense of change in the immediate environment but I could definitely sense that something was coming towards me or more to the point...to the scrape. It was the owner of the small patch of torn up ground forty yards up wind of the tree that I was perched in. He was a nice sized eight pointer, nothing in the wow stage but he was on my property, the place where I had first learned to hunt. It was the property which I had transformed, with knowledge acquired by years of hard work and asking a lot of questions, into a proper honey hole. All those lessons were now walking up the trail towards me to the set up that I had learned by reading articles. The only thing that would have made this more satisfying would have been if I had my hooky bow with me. Alas the scrape was too far from a suitable tree for a bow shot. The buck stopped under the licking branch and began to work the scrape. With his attention held by his task, it would have been easy to draw a bow on him. The fact that it was such an easy shot for a rifle did not take away much of the satisfaction. I eased my gun from its holder, slowly brought it to my shoulder laid the crosshairs on his vitals and then squeezed off the round. I had just taken my first buck on my own property. He fell in his tracks. I gave him a fair amount of time to be sure he was dead but there would be no tracking on this hunt. I just sat there and took it all in. It was an easy wait. I knew he was down for good. I knew he was an eight pointer, and that I would not have to look for him. I simply sat there and basked in self-satisfaction. When I finally lowered my gun and gear and got down to retrieve my prize that all too familiar sense of somber returned. I squatted beside him and thanked God for making me a hunter and for allowing me to harvest one of His animals. That moment passed, and I set about putting the buck in my truck and hauling him out to Balenacre. I cleaned him out and then hung him in the cooler so that he would be delicious when the time was right. It was the best meat I have ever eaten.

Jey was never able to get a bead on the magnificent buck during the rut. He kept trying but after the allure of mating was passed, he quickly went back to his sensible self and disappeared for the remainder of the season. I was glad that I left him alone on that stormy day. I had already had my chance with him last season. It was Jey's turn. Besides, I doubt that I could have gotten more pleasure taking "him" than I had received by taking my first buck on my own land. The property which I had developed myself, with my newly learned skills. I was getting it!

MISSISSIPPI BURNING

The deer season ended without too much more action. I got my three a year minimum so there would be venison for the next year. I tried my hand at turkey hunting again that spring. (Without Vernon) Rest assured I would not be successful without some help. Before we went into the fall season, we had planting to do. The fields all needed to be cut, burned, plowed and planted. It's an enjoyable time of year for me. I do like farming. Cutting all of them was no problem. I took care of that prior to our scheduled workday so we would be ahead of the game. Neither Joe nor Earnest could make it, so we were left with the bare minimum for burning...three, Vernon Jey and myself. We dutifully checked the weather for the day. Everything was favorable, so we contacted the forestry service for a burn permit. We wrote down the data that they relayed about wind speed and directions for the day. They issued the permit and work began. Each field was disked around three passes to create a fire-break. Then we would go to the upwind side of the field and pour a mixture of diesel fuel and burnt motor oil out at the corners. After checking with one another we would light the field. We then would follow the flame from one end of the field to the other as the wind pushed it gently along. At the other end we would meet it with shovels and dirt (from the disking) and extinguish the remnants of the fire. Two of us would go and prepare the next field. The third would police the field and make sure all was well before moving on to start the process again. The watch could take anywhere from one to two hours depending on the wind and general conditions of the field. Under no cir-cumstances would the next field be started until the last person had joined the party. That was always our plan and we always stuck to it.

Everything was going along quite well. By mid-day we were through three fields and preparing to start on the fourth. Vernon and I went to prep the fourth field. Jey sat with the one that we had just finished burning. By the time we moved the tractor to the barrel field and then disked the three circles around it the wind had picked up a lot. A whole lot and it had clocked 180 degrees. This was not in the wind predictions given by the forestry service at all. We reassessed the situation and decided to halt the burning for the rest of the day. It just wasn't safe anymore. I went inside and started on some lunch while Vern went back to the last field and informed Jey of our decision to stop. He came back and said Jey would be up in a little bit. He came back to the cabin a little bit later and we discussed what else we could do with the rest of the day that didn't involve fire. The whole time during our lunch discussion the wind continued to build. By the time we were finished it felt as though we were in a gale without the rain. I walked out of the cabin to check it out and saw the smoke. It was coming in the direction of the last field. "Fire" I yelled the other two came running out of the cabin and saw what I meant. Vernon said "I'll call the forestry and fire departments and you two go see what can be done. I'll come up with the tractor and disk as quickly as I can. It might come in handy." We jumped on the four-wheeler and raced back to the field. What we saw was beyond belief. The fire had formed a semi-circle in the trees around the field. It was burning all the underbrush and threatening to light the pine tree canopy. We attacked the fire with our shovels and the dirt piled up from our disking. We were making pretty good headway when Vernon arrived and joined in the fight. Just when it looked like we had it finally beat an incredibly strong gust of wind hit. The fire reacted as though someone hit the cutting handle on a blow torch. I could actually hear it screaming at me! All holy hell broke loose after that. I lost sight of my friends through the smoke and flames. Fire was everywhere. It was all around me and I didn't know where my friends were. I held my ground for reasons that I could not later explain. At one point I was surrounded by a circular wall of fire. The heat had caused my Kenny Chesney hat to explode into flames on my head. God was with me for sure because the wind shifted back in the other direction and took the flames with it. When the firemen got to where I had made my stand, they found a half-crazed man...tears in his eyes, singed hair and skin...red from the heat. I was beating out flames with a shovel in one hand and the tee shirt I had ripped off my back in the other. Two of them literally pulled me back while the rest started on the inferno with the fire hoses. They got me off the front lines, but I pressed my hand with them to continue to help. Seeing quickly that I wasn't going to give in they let me help with the fire hoses. Moving them to wherever they were needed so the trained people could do their stuff. And do they did. Those guys are great! What heroism. They all deserve a lot more credit than they get. They finally got the upper hand even though the wind continued to give them fits. While helping from the second line, I was able to see what I had just been through. Fully geared for fire with two and three hoses going the firemen were beating the flames back almost to a point of submission when the wind would suddenly gust up and temporarily envelope them before they would wet it down yet again. I could hear the anguished howls of the monster as it fed on the trees and was fueled by the wind. I watched the firemen fight it back again and again until it finally admitted defeat and suc-cumbed to the water and their efforts.

In the aftermath I found my friends alive and well...or as well as could be expected. I had lost all track of time during the inferno. We began to each give our account on the events prior to the fire to the authorities. I recall answering the fire chief's"... "What the hell were you thinking" question. "Trying to fight back a blaze like that with a shovel and your shirt! Are you crazy?" "I love this land" I answered defiantly! I noticed Vernon's wife in the crowd staring at me as though I was a crazy person. How could she have had time to get out to the farm? It had only been maybe a half hour or so since the fire started! And why was it so dark? Was it the smoke? No, the sun was going down! How could that be...it was only 12:30 or 1:00 tops! In actuality it was closer to 9:00. We had been in battle for almost eight hours. During most of that time my friends had no idea where I was. To me we had only been apart for a few moments at best. I had not had time to worry about them. Suddenly I was very tired, exhausted even. Johan was handing me a shirt that was two sizes too small. I slid it over my soot covered charred torso and we began to walk back to the cabin.

"Wait, there's still fire burning" I yelled! "No Mark, that's not wildfire" said a defeated sounding Vernon, "it's just the fence poles still burning. They're treated with creosote and will probably burn all night." We walked the rest of the way back to the cabin. Vern said goodnight to his wife then we all cleaned up and crashed. Nothing was said. There was nothing worth saying at that moment. We were all still alive! It would be months before we finally talked about it to one another. It was that painful to us all.

But again, all three friends were still quite alive and really that's all that mattered.

In the end, we were exonerated of any wrongdoing in the blaze. The official report cited extreme wind conditions for reigniting the smoldering roots of the fescue grass in the field we had been burning. No blame could be found in any of our actions. "The fescue's roots would have smoldered harmlessly for hours if the wind had not rekindled them. They were completely out of sight. No one could have known that there was any hint of danger involved in leaving the field which to all visible signs was extinguished."

That was the last field that was ever burned off at Balenacre.

*The burning of fields prior to planting is and will remain an excellent way to clear them of grass and weeds before disking. Whatever your plans after burning, the fire will help to assure that the crops are relatively free of unwanted extras. If you utilize this method, by all means follow all of the precautionary measures. While this will not assure that your blaze will not get out of control, it will greatly limit the chances of such a mishap. As it is with cooking, warmth or even a romantic glow, fire is good. **It must be respected at all times.** I have utilized* *field burning on other pieces of property since the incident at Balenacre with positive results, but the memory still haunts me, and I am even more careful than we were on that fateful day.*

*What I did that day to fight the fire may look heroic to some, but I am here to tell you now that it was positively **FOOLISH! Once a flame is deemed to be out of your control, retreat! Get out of its way! It has no respect for you. It does not care whether you have a wife and children or a mother. It can and will kill you.***

***Always obtain a burn permit if you are planning on using fire to clear a field.** It's the right thing to do. It's also the law. Doing so can protect you legally in case of a mishap. Also, in doing so, you will obtain valuable information which will ultimately make your efforts safer.*

***Always have the proper amount of manpower to safely compete the task at hand.** Not having enough people on the ground to control a burn is the best way to end up in a bad situation.*

***Always have a safe game plan for your burn and stick to it.** Include means to extinguish the fire as an integral part of that plan.*

***Keep the number for the forestry service as well as the local fire departments with you while you are working.** If a fire gets out of* control, call the authorities **_immediately_**. *They are not around to scold you or find fault in your procedures; they're there to help in the event of an emergency. Give them a fair chance to help you by not waiting until it's too late.*

*   **You'll never get a burn permit in the middle of a drought so if you're following the first rule, then you won't need this one.** Never start a fire in a drought.*

*   Some time later, I learned about the pain my actions had caused Johann. Years before, she had lost a very close cousin in the infamous "Man Gulch Fire". He and an entire team of well trained "Fire Jumpers" had perished heroically trying to do their jobs. Fire is indeed a dangerous entity! We were fortunate!*

BACK TO KENTUCKY

E ventually the aftermath of the fire subsided although it would be a long time indeed before the subject was no longer a tender one. Joe touched on the subject one evening by saying to me "well one possible good thing that might come out of the mishap is you might be able to finally find that pistol of yours." (The fire had started in the pistol field) Joe wasn't teasing me but rather trying to ease the pain some. Even so it didn't sit all that well. Another night Earnest thought enough time had passed to write a new nickname under Jey's tag on the sign in board, proclaiming him "the Firestarter"! That one went over like a bowling ball in a crystal shop! "That isn't a damned bit funny" yelled the "wookie"! "That wasn't his fault at all, and you know it." "He was just fooling around" said the big guy. "He didn't mean anything by it." "Yea, I was just kidding" chimed in Earnest. I accepted the apology, and we smartly dropped the subject.

As we began to resume our hunting plans for the season. It was very obvious that every time we were at the farm for whatever reason there were reminders of our ordeal. The most in your face was any time you went by the pistol field it was burnt to a crisp. The easy solution was just don't go near it then you won't see it. The reminder you could not avoid was the constant smell. Every time that the wind was blowing towards you, the charred smell of fire was in your nostrils. It became such a thorn that none of the three of us wanted to be out there. To quench our burning desire to hunt, we began to plan another trip to Kentucky. This trip was planned for the end of October.

As the planned trip drew near, we both paid more and more attention to the opportunity to hunt someplace where reminders of the fire were not in our faces or noses. Thinking about going back to Kentucky helped to ease the pain of the burnt area at and around the farm. Finally, the day arrived when we started packing up the truck and prepared to head back to "Booner Land". We were off to the farm at Mammoth Cave. We were both finally ourselves again, talking about the about hunts in their family's past and those to come. Vernon had me in stiches telling me stories about his family's hunting history. Stories about people like one of his cousins, who came up every year and went into the woods dragging an aluminum ladder. Vern mimicked the sounds a ladder would make as it was dragged through the woods banging into trees rocks and bushes. Then before long every year BAANG!!! His cousin would kill another giant deer. Then more ladder noises as he pulled his home-made portable stand back to the farm before heading back out with another family member to retrieve his animal. There were more stories about his dad casually showing up at just the right moment and wacking another one out from under the brother's noses. The funniest of the tales seemed to be ones about Vernon and his older brother Pat. Most of which seemed to end with smelling salts. The memory of the fire at Balenacre faded away and was replaced by laughter and excitement. We were finally there, and the magic of the place took over again. We were transported back in time to an era where the fabled frontiersmen of the great state were almost there with us. Electricity in the cabin seemed to be the only thing that separated us from them. Well, that and maybe fringed buckskins, moccasins and coon skinned caps. Even cold morning trips down to the outhouse only seemed to add to the mystic of the place. Each of the hunts we went on, morning noon and evening were the same hunts we went on anywhere else. Does came and went, bucks followed them in and then ultimately left only to be replaced by a different group of does and bucks at another location. None of the bucks were the one that we were looking for. In Kentucky you only get to take one buck...no more, so you don't get the luxury of a do over a few days later when the really big guy shows up. So, I was letting bucks beyond anything I'd ever encountered pass. Just enjoying the show. I watched them pass and continuing to wait. There were two differences from any of the other hunts I'd ever been on. First of course was the sense that at any given moment the "mediocre" bucks who were checking out the does could be replaced by a giant buck. I must add that the term "mediocre" is quite literally relative. These animals were far larger than any I had ever seen with the exception of the ten-pointer from the year before. And the second difference was that these bucks weren't just kind of nudging the does a little bit, they were really chasing them...hard! This was a real rut, like the ones you read about or see on hunting videos. The does were sweaty and lathered up, haggard and the bucks were hacked off at any of them who weren't receptive to them. It was the fabled RUT! My first ever and it was an incredible show!

After one of our morning hunts, I met up with Vernon around the road that led to the Cave Research Center. We began to walk/scout our way back to the cabin for a late breakfast. When we reached the field where I had let the buck walk the year before, there was a lone doe munching on a Halloween pumpkins innards. So absorbed in the delightful treat was she that she didn't even notice the two of us. She was about forty yards away from us and not a bit nervous about our presence. I assured Vernon that I could make the shot, so it was on. I moved closer to her to get myself in the acceptable range of about 30 yards. The shot was through a thin line of woods which is what separated us from her. I positioned myself, steadied myself and then went into auto-pilot mode. I drew back on her got her in my sites and loosed an arrow at her. The shot went through the woods, arced upwards as it would have to shoot that distance but then struck a twig at the height of its arc.

It was just enough to wreck my well-aimed shot which then landed three feet behind the hungry doe. To her it was just another twig that had fallen out of a tree. To me it was a lesson learned about how an arrow flies to its target. To Vernon it was an opportunity to laugh at the wookie. All three of us took it in stride. Vernon laughed, I learned, and the doe kept on eating her pumpkin pie. That's right she stayed in place eating. Did I say that "I Learned?" Well, everything in life is relative. I pulled another arrow from my quiver and lined up for another try. This time I tried to compensate for the arc of the shot by kneeling on one knee. This time it was not the tree branch that deflected my shot but the tall grass I was kneeling in. Once again, another twig interrupted the doe's brunch, once again I learned another lesson about arrow flight and once again Vernon got the opportunity to laugh at the wookie. The doe decided that the restaurant she was dining in was too disruptive for her liking and casually moved off. Vernon eventually stopped laughing at me and we moved off as well. When we got to the next break in the thin tree line, there she was again. This time it was Vernon who pulled the arrow from my quiver for me. Again, I guesstimated her range at 30 yards. By now my confidence was shaken...well that's my story, or maybe the lack of a range finder is my story who knows...anyway, I missed again. That was my last arrow, so the humiliation was apparently over. Not so. The doe moved up another twenty or so yards and started in on some acorns. Vernon crept over and retrieved the second arrow I had shot. He brought it back to me and said, "try again, this is fun". Now a normal man would have just let it go...after all three strikes and you're out right? Who has ever used the word normal in the same sentence with me? (Unless the prefix "ab" was also in the sentence). I tried again and missed again, Vernon laughed again, and the deer finally left the area. Perhaps I was grateful... at least it ended "that" part of the razzing! Thankfully they were happy with the name "dad's field" or they might have re-named it the porcupine field or some such other humiliating reminder of the morning's event. Years later, while brush hogging the field, Pat fount one of my lost arrows.

I'm a southern boy through and through. There's not much of anything that I think is better than being down south. That said, the Deep South does not produce the same caliber of rut activity that you'll find up north or out west. Conditions just don't force deer to compete for mating rights as aggressively as in other parts of the country. As such if you ever get the opportunity to observe a more traditional aggressive rut, don't pass on it. Indeed, it is something to behold. Seeing that activity firsthand compares with most of the better hunting situations I've been on.

There were a lot of lessons packed into the porcupine field incident. Most of them revolved around knowing the trajectory of an arrow once it's been fired. An arrow, or a bullet for that matter does not just fly straight until it runs out of momentum. They arch upwards and then reach a zenith and begin to fall slowly at first back down. The more velocity they lose, the faster they begin to fall. That lesson never really sank in for me until that humorously fateful day. As I repeatedly launched arrows at the unsuspecting doe, the point was driven home. First the tree branches deflected its path, and then the tall grass did the same. Remember in the "Waiting for the Bus" story when "Neos" arrow stopped in midair while seemingly on its way to the first kill with the hookie bow? Not looking where the arrow would have to fly to reach its target *was the cause of that. The same holds true with tiny branches that are part of your cover. Always know what your bullet or arrow must fly through before you pull the trigger. If you don't, you may find yourself staring at an empty field while your target runs off to safety, or far worse, blood trailing a wounded animal.*

Spelunking

Later in the week, Vernon's son Justin showed up from his first year of college. We enjoyed some hunts together and some cool memories with the other family members. Ultimately, we decided it was time for a new adventure. There was a really cool cave located on the family farm. I had been told tales of years past where it had been explored by different people. It was said that there was a subterranean waterfall near what was thought to be the back of the cave. Now being an avid cave diver, I was highly interested in not only seeing the falls, but also exploring where all that water came from and where it went from there. My explorer gene was in high gear with visions of making the next trip with my cave diving gear, but alas no one would enter the cave with me. No one until Justin arrived on the scene! Justin was now in his bulletproof years and "twern't scared of nothing." We agreed to forego the morning's hunt in lieu of a greater quest. The fountain of foolishness! I haven't done a lot of spelunking, but I assumed that a lot of the same rules that held true for cave diving applied for the aforementioned as well. Best of all, I thought, you don't have to keep a watch on your air supply. How hard could it be? REALLY??? Won't I Ever Learn? Well, I gathered some rope, flash lights, a little bit of water and oh yeah, Vernon's camera. Down the rabbit hole we went. Literally, the entrance to the cave was about a forty foot almost vertical drop. We worked our way to the cave floor and the first thing we were greeted with was the carcass of a deer fawn that had fallen in. Now I know that we kill deer when we hunt but this was tragic. If the little fellow survived the fall, what a terrible death. And how about its poor mother. No way to help it out. It was a very sad start to our adventure. What it should have been was a warning. We began our exploration. Marking our movement so we could find our way out later. We followed the general idea of where we had been told that the waterfall was supposed to be. After maybe twenty minutes we began to hear water. Our excitement grew, and we pressed on continuing to mark our trail in as we went. The sound grew louder as we progressed. It began to sound almost ominous, but we kept going. Then the sound grew loud enough that the echoing in the cave almost made the noise hurt. I could sense the moisture in the air and a type of misty cloud materialized. Finally, there it was! It wasn't as big as we'd been led to believe. Or perhaps the more truthful statement is that it wasn't as big as we'd imagined. It dropped from the rock above no more than ten or so feet. We had little to climb with so that option wasn't happening, but as best we could tell, the only opening in the rock was the size of the falls themselves. No way a person could fit through there even without cave diving gear. The pool it dropped into worked its way off to the left. We followed the movement of it until it fell through an opening that likewise a person could not fit through. None the less, I dropped down into the cold stream got a deep breath and plunged my head into the hole. I could see the stream tumbling downwards and further off to the left but with no waterproof light and no mask that was about all I could take in. So much for diving it! As we had been told, that did appear to be the end of that part of the cave, so we started back exploring the many off shoots along the way. We decided that we would investigate some of the shoots. As long as a space big enough to turn around in was visible, then we would go forth and check it out. We were having a ball doing so. I had studied geology in college and would have majored in it had drop add not been an easier curriculum. That said, I knew enough about the formations to pass some of my schooling on to Justin. He found one hole that went a long way in. Far enough that I lost sight of him. It had been agreed that only one of us would explore the side treks while the other stayed at its entrance. I called him back. He came back and told me that this one went a good way back and was pretty cool. We swapped places and I went in. The cave led to a fissure in the wall that went up maybe thirty feet. Stupidly I put my back against one wall and my feet against the other and walked my way up to the top. I called down from my perch to a startled Justin whom I could see from the mini cliff. We had a good laugh and then I worked my way back down and came back. On and on we went with our exploration. We were taking pictures and video so we could share our experiences with the others. It was great fun and we completely lost track of time. Justin located another inter-esting hole. It was a vertical drop straight down through a small hole. I held on to Justin's feet and lowered his head down into the opening so he could look around with his flashlight. "WOW" he exclaimed. "This one's way beyond cool". I pulled him back out and began to discuss it with him. "It's maybe five feet down to the floor and then it goes back the way we just came" he said. Could you see a turnaround spot" I asked? "No need" he answered, "It's really wide down there". We agreed that it was too cool not to look further into so as before I would stay at the top and he would get to explore it. It kept going and going and like the energizer bunny so did Justin. He went on to the point that I could barely hear his voice and I called "NO JOY". He dutifully came back and told me about the lower cave. It was as wide as the one we were in. You could stand up completely in some places and stoop to move forward in others. This one I couldn't pass up. I lowered my legs down through the hole up to my arm pits. My shoulders and arms wouldn't fit the opening together, so I raised my arms over my head and slid through to the floor below. All this on film! I returned his earlier "WOW" statement with one of my own. It was off to the races for me. His description was near perfect. Further and further, I moved through the cave until I hit the same spot that he had been in where he could barely hear me and vice versa. He called "NO JOY" and reluctantly I made my way back to the hole. When I got there, we had a conversation about what we had encountered for a few minutes before I decided to get out. I was a lot bigger than Justin at the time, (Not anymore) so him throwing me a hand and pulling me out as I had done for him was not happening. I put my arms back over my head, jumped just a little so they were free of the hole and spread them out on the floor above me. "Cool" said Justin as he kept the video camera running for prosperity's sake. All I had to do now to gain freedom was to press down on the floor above me and raise my torso out of the hole. Uh Oh! As I pushed up, my well defined lat muscles expanded to the point that they wouldn't make it through the opening. I dropped back to my starting point and tried again. Same results. All this on film. Just then I hear Justin say "STUCK?" ... I answered back "STUCK!" "What do we do?" he asked. "For starters, turn off that recorder" I said. "OK, now what?" he asked after the infernal truth teller was shut down. "Well," I said "it's for sure I'm not fitting through using both arms, so I'll have to do it with one." That didn't work either, because as I pushed with one arm, my body went into the opposite wall of the opening with equal force and once again stopped me. "Ok that didn't work" he said, "now what?" "Give me your hand" I said. He did, and I pulled with one hand to free myself. All that did was pull Justin towards me like a leaf. "Now what?" he said with just a hint of fear in his voice. I was having the same feeling creeping up on me but knew from years of cave diving that it wasn't gonna help matters at all to give into it. "Let's try this" I offered, "lay down on your belly and grab that rock in front of you and HANG ON. I'm gonna grab on to your feet with one hand and pull myself out." Fortunately, that's exactly what happened. I was free, thank God! We agreed that was enough for one day. We followed our trail out, climbed back up the entrance with the rope we'd left there and our adventure in the cave was over. Before we started back to the cabin, we took a good look at each other. There is no descriptive word in the English language for how dirty we both were. At least none that I know of. We decided to take a quick peak at a little of the footage we'd captured. The camera that Vern had let me borrow was trashed. It was caked in the same grimy mixture that we had all over us. So bad was it that the auto focus lens wouldn't budge... in, or out. After all we had done that morning...now is when panic struck! "Dad's gonna kill us" said Justin! "No, I said, "your dad's gonna kill me. I'm the one who borrowed it" "My dad's gonna Kill us" he repeated sounding a bit like Spacolli's friend in Fast Times. "We'll fix it" I said not exactly sure how, since my dad's "awesome set of tools" was several hundred miles away and not meant to work on cameras. We managed to find some cloth clean enough to work on it and eventually got it clean enough to be called filthy. The other good news was that the lens now worked again, and you could see the video on the screen. We sheepishly took it back and hoped for the best. When we approached him at first he was so shocked at our appearance that he was taken a back. That led to a kind of joy that we were back. That was enough of an opening for me and the camera dilemma. I did my best sales pitch on him, showed it to him and all was forgiven. Justin and I worked on it for a few hours and got it back to good as new status. We then gathered the brothers out on the front porch and began to share our adventure with them. We all started looking at scenes from the cave both brothers had explored as kids. The laughter started and we became more focused on our antics. Gradually the laughter lessened. Not because of lack of humorous acts on our part, but from lack of an audience. One at a time both Pat and then Vernon had quietly exited the porch. The video Justin had shot was so graphic and vivid that they had both succumbed to the effects of Closter phobia.

The spelunking story doesn't really have anything to do with hunting. The only reason I included the story is because it was a big part of that hunting trip to Kentucky that year. Other than being a great story, it did open some areas about following safety guidelines. Exploring anything can be exciting and fun. Caving is certainly no exception to that rule of thumb. That said, caving is inherently dangerous. Even a simple cave can be problematic if you are not properly trained. The cave in this story was anything but simple. Justin and I were lucky. We got in, explored had fun and GOT OUT UNHARMED! Many novice cavers don't. Some don't make it out at all. Spelunking is very rewarding, but if you're going to do it, acquire training and the proper gear. I relied on my cave diving training for our entrance into that cave. Some of that training, like marking your trail crossed over to spelunking very well. Other things did not. For instance, you don't usually need a rope in cave diving. The only rope we took with us was used and left at the entrance to the cave, so we were left without one. A definite no no in spelunking... Again, Get Training if you're gonna do it.

As wonderful as it all was, no deer were taken, and we finally ran out of time. There were plenty of new stories to add to the family hearth collection and there were several good encounters, and every hunt was magical, but no deer lost their lives to us that season. That doesn't by any way shape or form mean that it was an unsuccessful hunt. We had gotten almost everything we came for once again.

I was mistaken when I said no deer lost their lives to us that season. Just no Kentucky deer died. We all had another good season at Balenacre, even with the reminders of the fire all around us. We were all finally resolved that we had done nothing wrong, and it had been beyond our control. The pain was finally lessoning. Good friends enjoyed more good times with good stories to match and it culminated in each of us taking home more fantastic meat to show for it. That meat was shared with guests in our homes who learned more about who we were and how that feast before them came to be.

That spring Vernon announced that he was going to put the farm on the market. Everyone in the club took that news pretty hard. The place had become part of our DNA. It was a big part of who we were. But it was not our property. For myself the news was met with full-fledged depression. For a good while I couldn't bring myself to even go out there. I missed turkey season because of it. Big bird expert that I had become. Ultimately, I realized that was just stupid. Vernon kept saying that "it's time to move on". Maybe he was ready, but I wasn't. He did convince me that the farm might take a while to sell and that it would need to be kept up during that time span and he could use my help. That worked. Things almost went back to normal for a good while except now it was just he and I going out there. The guys in the club had seen this all before and were used to it. They were able to do what I was not...move on! For a while I lived in the false hope that it would not sell. Then I realized that was NOT what my FRIEND wanted to have happen. As a GOOD FRIEND, I came to grips with the whole thing. Some good did come out of it eventually. Ultimately a lot of good came out of it.

We worked on projects, just like before. We maintained the roads and stands, planted, hunted, fished. We entertained guest's, cut up, laughed and every once in a while, even drank a cold beer. The only things that had changed was that the farm was on the market, and that the rest of the gang wasn't out there nearly as much. That was really the worst of it. These guys had all been there when I was cutting my "hunting" teeth. They had become extended family in my new lifestyle, and I missed them a lot. That said, not having them around all the time was also a blessing in disguise. I was now in a position where I could begin to spread my hunting wings so to speak. Maybe hunting legs would be a better description. I was able to spread out. I was able to walk around, and move in and out of stands at will without infringing on anyone else's territory. I began to experiment with the art of still hunting. Being on the ground and moving towards your intended game instead of waiting in ambush for it to come to you. While there is certainly nothing at all wrong with that, I would have never tried still hunting had the guys been around. Change had forced me into a new and exciting world. Just like moving from junior high school on to high school. One was good for one set of reasons, while the other was good for a whole new different set of them. All that said, I had a lot more learning to do before I would be able to say that I had mastered still hunting. As that new season of learning continued, Vernon once again invited me to go back to Kentucky with him. Of course, I declined...NOT!

This next trip was planned towards the end of October around the pre-rut. We had agreed that it would be a bows only trip. Once again, we began to gather up our gear and prepare ourselves mentally for yet another adventure in the land of giants. This time we drove separately. Vernon came up early for a class reunion while I had to tend to some unfinished business first before I could enjoy the trip. Also, sadly the family had lost Charles earlier in the year. We met at the family house so they could work together on the affairs of the estate. Pat took me down to the cellar to show me the massive deer that he had taken the year before after we had left. What a magnificent animal. They finished up with their duty while I packed up and left for the farmhouse at Mammoth Cave. All I could talk about was the size of Pat's deer. Once again I entered the ancient almost one lane road that separated the Park from their cabin. I was again in the land of the giants...

stoked wasn't a sufficient phrase but it would have to do. I got to camp a couple of days before Bwana. Pat joined me later that evening. He's a super nice guy, a gentle giant who I would never want to have mad at me. We hung out, told stories, watched old movies and scouted. He knew more about the property and the land surrounding it than the game wardens in the area did. He also knew them well. Called them his friends. Pat had been talking with one of them and had been told of a Boone & Crocket buck who made the area on the edge of the game reserve his home. The next place from his bedroom was the family's farm. It was on! I was finally hunting in an area that was known to have a record book buck close...Very close! I did some gentle scouting while I was waiting on my buddy to show up. When he did, in true Balenacre fashion, I shared with him every-thing I had learned scouting. We would start the hunt the next day. I had already put up stands where I thought the hunting would be best. Vernon agreed with most of my choices and had reasons for the few he didn't like. After the morning hunt we would move those together. Sleep came easy after a few pulls from the Wild Turkey bottle we had.

We awoke early the next morning dressed, grabbed our gear which was already sorted out according to our needs the night before. We were out the door and on the way to our stands well before daybreak. There was deer movement from the start, I found out later it was the same for Vernon. There were does and small bucks, it was all very exciting but there were no signs of the big bucks we had come for. What was exciting was the indicators that the rut was about to begin. The youngsters were definitely starting to harass the does even if they weren't receptive yet. We were in the Promised Land at the perfect time for an interview with a legend.

For those of you who have never had the opportunity to hunt in a place where an incredible animal can show up at any time, I will feebly attempt to describe the electricity in the air for the hunts to come. I'm going to take the liberty that most you readers have been hunting in a stand where you've been for several hours and seen nothing. You're thinking about either moving to another location or perhaps giving up all together when...in back of, you there comes the familiar sound of footsteps in the leaves...

"crunch crunch crunch... crunch crunch crunch"! Now at this point, your imagination and other senses are telling you that a 140 class twelve pointer is in back of you moving slowly towards a spot where you've diligently cut out a shooting lane. "Crunch crunch crunch, he's right in back of you now! You don't dare turn around to get a peek at him because he'll catch you moving and bolt before you can your chance at him. You know in your soul that it's the buck you've been looking for all season, maybe even your whole life and you can't even steal a quick look! Your heart rate would scare your doctor into his own heart attack. Every ounce of your being is alive! More alive than you've ever been! More aware of your surroundings than you ever were before! You turn your existence over to your animalistic instincts and it shifts to auto pilot. More slowly than is humanly possible under any other set of circumstances your body begins to turn towards the sounds of your invader. Inch by inch, your whole body moves as one unit. After twenty or so minutes (real time perhaps only two minutes) you've managed to rotate so that you can finally see the animal you've dreamt of...

That moment can be many things. It could indeed have been the buck you were searching for. It may have only been a doe or perhaps a spike. It could have even been a man-eating squirrel. The fact is that for the one instant, prior to actually seeing what had made the noise that "awakened you," it did not matter what the perpetrator was. Buck, doe, fawn or the terrifyingly deadly squirrel; you were more alive at that moment than description allows and THAT my friends is why we hunt!.

Now let's shift back to Kentucky, back to the farm where massive bucks had been taken two of the past three years. Every sound, every movement of every moment you're out in the woods is the exact same feeling as the moment described in the paragraph above. Just like it was as you were trying to turn and get a look at that buck, but not only for an agonizingly exciting two minutes, every moment from the time we walked out of that rustic old cabin until we took our boots off as we went back in. ELECTRIC that's as good a description as any. Every hunt was like that, even the time spent inside was different. There was a more alert air about the place. We had one great hunting day after another. Plenty of deer were sighted, even some really nice bucks. Knowing both that you could only take one and that the "One of a lifetime" was in the immediate area...well it changed things. I think for the better.

Vernon was running out of time because he had to get back to South Carolina for some other commitments. Pat lived there and wasn't going anywhere, and neither was I! The last night he was there, Vernon took a nice doe so that he wasn't going home with no meat. I helped him gather her in and ready her for the trip home. We threw the cork away on the Rare Breed bottle and celebrated his last night there. The next morning, he was off to South Carolina. I headed off for another of the now "normal rut encounters" I had become accustomed to...or so I thought!

Area "Fifty-Two"

Pat had convinced me that the field right behind the cabin was the best place to go for the big buck that the game warden had told him about. I had been going to all the remote places as far away as I could get because I was sure that the big guy would never make it that easy on me. Pat knew more than I did and I knew it so I relented and took his advice. This was the exact same field where I had erroneously let the big ten-pointer walk two years before. I took my climber down the valley to a thin grove of trees that grew in a small ravine. It separated two parts of the same field. It was the same thin grove of trees that I had tried unsuccessfully the year before to shoot through at the doe eating pumpkin innards. The thin grove ended as did the fields at a much heavier line of trees which bordered the road that led to the cave research center. The way the two tree lines converged formed a kind of "T" with the trees I was in being the stem and the ones bordering the road as the top of that "T". It was a fantastic set up. From where I was hidden, I had the field to either side of the funnel to shoot into as well as the ravine I was set up in. The only disadvantage to my set up was that the heavier woods that formed the top of the "T" were about fifty yards away. Fifty-two to be exact. I know because I ranged it at least that many times during the rest of my hunt.

I had only been in the stand for about fifteen minutes when I began to hear a commotion in the woods by the road. It was just some rustling at first, but it began to grow in its intensity over the next ten agonizing minutes. It was still dark, and I could only hear what was going on. The best description I can come up with was that it sounded like a bulldozer crashing through the shrubs...with its engine off! I was beside myself! The most intense action I had seen (well heard anyway) yet and I was going to miss it all because the sun wasn't up! I used all my telepathic powers (of which I have none) to will the sun into the sky so I could see what I was hearing. Finally, the sun gave in to my overwhelming superhuman powers... or maybe to the regularity of a normal sunrise, who can say for sure, but it finally did. Doing so the light unveiled the carnage before me. There was only one doe. She looked as though she had been chased by the afore mentioned bulldozer all night! She was sweaty, her coat looked as if it had been brushed backwards by some unseen demonic fairy. She could barely stand she was so exhausted! The "bulldozer" she had been trying to evade all night was the biggest buck I have ever seen. I don't just mean in person; I mean any and all the TV shows or hunting videos I have ever watched! Hold your hands up over your head as wide as you can make them go and you'll have some idea of what I'm talking about. He was a massive twelve pointer with plenty of mass and a body to match.

I somehow managed to find my range finder without falling out of the tree and then get it to my eyes without dropping it. Fifty-two yards! DAMN! I had made that shot hundreds of times... at targets! Yep exactly fifty-two yards... as I ranged it again, double damn! I lowered my range finder and brought my Steiner's up to my eyes and focused on the scene before me. The doe would try to lie down but her suitor would have none of it. He'd nudge her, push her, even bite her till she'd stand up then he'd chase her around the brush till she'd stand still long enough for him to mount her. That would last for a minute or so then they'd break off and the whole process would start again. Fifty-two yards! Damn! All that moving around, and they hadn't come one foot closer... yet. But I knew at any given moment the doe could trot my way for twenty yards and the bruiser would follow her. Did she have the energy to run that far? If she did, I knew he did. This went on for thirty minutes. Always in the same location, mowing over and bulldozing the same saplings and brush. Couldn't they tell that the area had been cleared and it was time to plow somewhere else? You know, somewhere CLOSER! Finally, the monster buck allowed the doe to lay where she had collapsed. He walked around looking in every direction for any signs of an intruder or a jealous husband. Finding none he too laid down beside her. At Fifty-Two yards!

The two of them settled down for a long winters nap... alright alright, it was fall so what! It wasn't a long nap either, perhaps only two hours. Let me ask you a question, how many full-blown arguments can you have (with your-self) over an in-depth subject in two hours? Do you get down and silently walk towards the exhausted couple...do you sit tight and leave well enough alone? Leave everything to fate?

Now this was a hunter who was still in transition. NOT the hunter whom at the preface of this book was able to use his skills to still hunt right past a sleeping buck in the crunchy leaves of a fall drought. The relative novice in the tree at this time had only seen a proper rut twice, and barely knew what still hunting was! "Still hunting", isn't that when you stay in the stand past when your fellow hunters have made it safely back to the cabin and one asks... "Are you (still) hunting???" I was not yet good enough to get down and stalk the two exhausted creatures of God who could bust a lowly human on their worst day... in their sleep! I did not yet know that such hunting could even be done. My instincts told me to get down and do what was natural. What I knew in my soul as a hunter, and what I had been taught as normal practice told me two different things... told me that the patient hunter is the one who triumphs. I listened to the latter. I stayed where I was and waited for them to wake from their slumber and then move towards my ambush point. I still had a lot to learn!

I did what I had been taught, I stayed where I was at. The spot where the two had no clue of my existence. Chances were good that they would wake and move towards me. Then

I would get a shot at the animal of my dreams. To quote my mother... "he who hesitates is lost" ok, that wasn't really 'her' quote but growing up, I didn't know that. They were only fifty-two yards away!

How long had I been up here? An hour? A few days? A week, a month? In reality, it was 8:30 (am) when signs of life started to present themselves again. The first, my heart was actually beating! At a countable rate! Next, movement! More so than just an occasional ear twitch or tail flicker...The doe stood up! My future prize stayed where he was, but she was now on her feet. From the way she was staggering I could tell that she needed nourishment. The buck... well all he needed was her. She began to move around. Browsing, looking for food as she moved...and she was moving slowly towards me! Her suitor stayed his ground, not moving but not missing anything she did. Not even a flick of her matted tail. She had slowly, almost by moving backwards inched ten yards closer to my hideout. The buck staggered up, shook off the cobwebs of an elongated night and in an almost imperceptible leap, cut the doe off from what must have looked to him like an attempted escape from Stalag 13. He herded her back to area fifty-two and began to defile her again.

So engrossed was I in the scene that was being put on for me fifty-two yards away that I failed to notice that I was not the only one at the movie theater watching the show. A slight movement to my left was enough break the magical spell I'd been under for the past three hours. I had failed to notice that another truly magnificent animal had joined my ranks and was watching the same show that I was with equal interest. A beautiful buck was just as intent on watching the buck harass his doe as me. Like me he wanted to be sure that the couple didn't notice his presence but for a totally different reason from mine. He didn't want to get his butt kicked by the 200 plus inch bruiser that I was trying to arrow.

He was a near perfect eight pointer. I sized him up estimating him to be around the 150-class range. He was the biggest buck that I had ever had a chance to shoot including the ten pointer I had not shot a few years before, and here he was twenty yards away from me. The wind wasn't 100 percent right, but it wasn't wrong either. He was turned broadside to me and was so focused on the other two deer that he hadn't a clue I was even there. I was now in the driver's seat. The choice was mine for the making; I could take a relatively easy 20-yard shot at the biggest buck I'd ever taken, or I could wait it out and have a once in a lifetime chance to try and take the biggest buck I would probably ever get the chance to take. What a wonderful dilemma to have...but it was still a dilemma none the less. The hourglass was turned over the minute I noticed the newcomer. The chance that he was going to try and challenge the bulldozer to a shoving match was pretty much nil. Him being as interested in the show as I was and being content to just hang out and just watch with me was just about the same. There was only gonna be so much time he would remain there and even less of it that he would be so preoccupied that he didn't notice me. I began to wonder if taking the bird in hand was indeed not a lot better than the two in the bush...the bush being exactly fifty-two yards away from me. In three hours', time, the giant whitetail had only for the very briefest of moments moved a few feet towards me and his ultimate demise. The incredible animal to my left wasn't gonna stay twenty feet away for that long. I made the decision that he was good enough. "GOOD ENOUGH"? He was by far the biggest deer I had ever had a chance at, and he was NOT 52 yards away. Suddenly "I wasn't in Kansas anymore" ...KANSAS? (I thought I was in Kentucky)! This was no longer a hypothetical situation where "what if" existed. I was now set in motion on taking the absolute biggest deer of my life... Twenty Yards Away! I very slowly turned my range finder on the newcomer. He was exactly 18 yards away and quartered slightly towards me. That made for a great shot, but it also put me in his direct line of sight in the only place in my set up that lacked decent cover. I stayed frozen on him with my range finder for I guess about a week...or maybe it was just a couple of minutes before he directed his attention back towards the action in area fifty-two. I used that moment to slowly lower my range finder. That was enough movement to bring his focus back in his own area. His mannerisms began to get jumpy. I knew he was now spooked. That made my job infinitely harder. At that moment a car came down the gravel road that divided the park from the property I was on. That was per-fect. It was something the big fella had heard throughout his life, so it didn't send him into over (as in my hunt was over) drive, but it did distract him long enough for me to quickly pick my bow up and get back into shooting position for what hopefully would be my next break. I stood perfectly still (except for my heart) and waited while the eight- pointer nervously shifted about. One more distraction and I could draw on the biggest deer of my life! Would he bolt? Would he look away long enough for me to draw and take aim? "PATIENCE!!! Don't panic" I silently told myself. I wasn't about to try and snapshot the biggest buck I'd ever been on. And yet he was so close to running. Everything I had learned about hunting up to this moment told me that everything in his actions indicated that he was ready to take flight. Still there was one more hard-earned hunting lesson I knew. You can sometimes take a snapshot with a recurve bow, but you can never make an accurate one with a compound bow. I wasn't about to try. I stayed there in that space in time for the longest minute in recorded history. Finally, I got the break I needed. The huge buck in area fifty-two had mounted his captive again and was letting out the loudest tending grunt I have ever heard. Not only did it get the buck back in my area's attention, but it also got mine. Suddenly I was focused on him again. I looked down the tree line to where they were. When I rightly turned my attention back to the bird in hand...I mean the buck eighteen yards away. In my own moment of distraction, I had failed to take advantage of the smaller buck's distraction by drawing on him. As I turned my attention fully back on him, he was now fully directed on me! He had caught some movement that I had made when I turned see what was happening in area fifty-two. We were now in eye-to-eye contact and that is never a good thing with a whitetail, unless he's on a wall. That was one place that this deer was not going to be. He spun on a dime and hightailed it (quite literally) for the park. I watched his white tail disappear from my sight which didn't take long at all. When I turned my attention back to area fifty-two, it was as vacated as the famed "Area Fifty-One" Either the smaller buck's dash for safety or more than likely some movement of my own had sent the couple on their own way never to be seen by me again. "That's Bow Hunting"! A rifle would have taken either one of them. No, not true. If I'd had a rifle, I would never have seen the second buck because I'd have shot the one in area fifty-two the moment I had shooting light.

Once again, I find myself in familiar territory. And again, I'm telling my readers about one of the best hunts I've ever been on. Once again, I didn't even take a shot. For the rest of my life,

I'll tell this story, wonder about what I should have done or about what I could have done differently. How many ways could I have changed the way I hunted that morning? How different the outcome might have been? I've already had dozens of friends and experts tell me what I should have done or what I did wrong. Guy's, you know what? I didn't do a thing wrong! There isn't a single thing about that hunt that needed a different ending. Nothing I could have done would have made it a better hunt. It was perfect! To date without a doubt the absolute best hunt...

You know what, they've all been good! The ones with good friends, and the ones where I was so alone my thoughts echoed. The special ones where I was able to share a first hunt with a new hunter. The ones with a great ending as well as the ones where I did something incredibly stupid. Even the ones where I got hurt. Every moment that I've spent in the field. Even the moments preparing a field. Preparing for a hunt. The time spent traveling to or from that hunt... ALL are special to me. Every single moment that I've labored dressing game that I've taken with my own hands, using the skills that good friends had taught me, or those I have learned on my own. Every hour in a

kitchen preparing a feast that... start to finish I created myself with my own...well everything. Entertaining guests at our home, allowing them to partake in the story behind the meal that they were enjoying at that moment. Sharing with them a mental picture to go along with the taste they were enjoying. Letting them feel a little of the effort it took, just a small portion of how that meal came to be. For just a moment in their lives they could understand what it meant to hunt. In that moment they could see...why we hunt, who we are and who they too could be. All without having ever taken a shot. Just like some of the best hunts I've ever been on.

All good things come to an end. While this is a very true statement there are things left out that are equally true. Vernon had put the farm on the market. That action kind of disbanded the club which was terrible. But some good had come of it. While the farm had been on the market it still needed to be kept up and that was too big a chore for any one person. Not wanting to lose contact with my buddy or Balenacre, I had volunteered to help him keep it up. So, things had already changed but still stayed the same. The chores I had grown to love were still in need of doing so they were done throughout that last summer. The leads he had on the sale had fallen through and summer had led into fall. The fields were planted to encourage the sale. It had turned to fall and so, well... we hunted it! With no one around whose hunts I could infringe on, I had begun to move about a lot more. It was during that last season at the farm that I had learned the art of still hunting. It became and still is my favorite way to hunt. Over the course of that season, I became proficient at it. Both the bucks I took that season were taken from the ground. I eventually became the hunter who was in the forward of this book...able to successfully stalk up a mountain in the crunchy leaves of a fall drought. Able to move quietly through the woods while paying attention to everything...the wind, the sign around me, tracks and the animals themselves. These were the skills that I had needed to have taken the massive Kentucky twelve pointer. After that season's end, I would have those skills whenever the opportunity presented itself again. And I have! This probably would have never taken place had Vernon not put his farm on the market. Once again change turned into something good.

Eventually Balenacre sold and we both found ourselves without a place to hunt. We found a club that needed some new members and joined that. New hunters with different hunting styles and new lands. In some cases, new property owners to learn how to interact with. New hunting grounds to figure out, lots of new acreage to figure out in fact. Turns out, there's a lot of land in this country in need of hunters. Finding this land is a new experience unto itself. Do you buy, do you lease, initiate a co-op... Public land hunting can be a wonderful experience. There are places all over that adventurous outdoorsmen can explore. New topography, new weather patterns, new species of tasty animals. A whole new world is out there for the taking. All the skills that I had been taught or learned myself over the years have paid out in huge dividends. While the magic of the fabled Balenacre never again emerged in full, new and exciting doors opened up by accepting and embracing change. That lesson has led me to new and wonderful hunting experiences. Translated into regular life it led me to do the same in a lot of other aspects of life most of which had positive outcomes.

Change is nothing to be afraid of! Quite the contrary, it can and often should be welcomed. You can't learn new things if you stay in the same rut for your entire life. It was most frightening to leave junior high school and then move on to high school. But what would happen if you didn't? In my case, the forced change at Balenacre also allowed me to become a far more advanced hunter. While the skills I learned at that first farm in my first seasons took me a long way both in hunting and in life-style, had I not changed, I would have never advanced. By having that taken away from me, it forced me to do what in all likelihood, I would never have done...evolve into something dif-ferent, something more complex...something more complete, more well-rounded...some-thing better!

"The Teacher Becomes The Student"

It had taken three years to finish a book that took me less than one to write. There were a lot of reasons for the delay. Writer's block, some who knew me and others who knew writing would say. Disillusionment was yet another reason. The truth is less palatable to me and while writing this I realize FAR more embarrassing to me than any of the stupid things I did while learning to hunt. I had convinced myself that however pleased I was with my compilation of stories, the public I was trying to reach needed to believe in my abilities as a woodsman in order to accept the lessons that went with them. How better to prove myself to be that than to accomplish something remarkable? I decided that the best form of acknowledgment would be to take a mighty deer with my bow. That animal with me on the cover of my book would give me the status I would need for it to be successful. Once again, I would wonder into the realm of trying to do something without asking for advice. Once again it ended poorly but with a valued lesson.

The first of those three years found me with pictures on my trail cams of a tremendous bruiser of a buck. I patterned the creature, found his bedding area, his food source and his travel patterns. With that information I formulated a plan. All these skills had been acquired over the years while learning to hunt. The "skill" I had not yet learned was hunting one single buck and no other...which was the road I found myself traveling down. It was early in the season. The bucks were still in bachelor groups and still in their summer feeding pattern. The massive eight pointer I was hunting was visiting a rub at ten to fifteen minutes before dusk regularly. He was always the last of the group to show up. There had been several opportunities to take other nice bucks, but I had opted to wait for "my buck". Several encounters occurred where he was in range of my bow. One where he was partially covered by brush. I probably could have taken him, but it was an uncertain and thus unfair shot. It was early in the season, and I was sure there would be other chances. The other was a stare down with him. It was later in the season but still pre-rut. It had been raining and the lesson learned long ago still proved to be accurate. As the rain lessoned, he showed up to what was now his scrape to freshen it up. He came in to do his thing as the rain tapered off. I had my climber well hidden in a tree 20 yards from the scrape. I had him and I knew it! As he approached, I stood and readied myself for the shot. As luck would have it a large drop of rain hit the umbrella I had screwed into the tree above me. Barely noticeable on any other occasion, at that moment, it was as loud as that shotgun blast in the truck trailer my first-year hunting. My quarry looked up towards the sound and noticed a rather odd bulge on the side of the tree. I froze and avoided eye contact with him. After a long wait, he dismissed the event...almost! He now played the head down head up game with me, almost giving me a chance to draw but then looking back up at the odd shape on the side of the tree. All this as the light continued to fade. By the time he'd relaxed enough for me to fix my lighted sight pin on his vitals, they were a darkened blur. I could have released and hoped for the best, but that was not who I'd become as a hunter. I made the fair and thus right decision and let him go. I waited until he left the area so as not to educate him of my presence and went home knowing that I was close and sure that I could still harvest him. I returned a few days later when the wind was favorable to continue my quest...what I found shook me to the core and disillusioned me beyond repair for the rest of the season. Tire tracks...my heart sank as I followed them to the ending that I already knew... POACHER'S! The tracks led through the woods straight up to the rubbed tree, which they had overrun. They had come in with a purpose... to pick up the deer they had poached. My buck. The "trophy" that I had been hunting for over a month. Dejected, disgusted and angry, I walked away for most of the rest of the season. I finally did pick up my bow towards the end of the season to harvest some much wanted and needed meat. As such I reacquainted myself with my passion without realizing that I had allowed another person to control the joy of the hunt.

That happened again the following year when a series of incidents within the club once again stole the joy of my passion from me. Rather if the truth be told, I allowed those incidents to consume me and thus take away that joy. Rules are Rules for All...and we All should make every attempt to follow them. That stated, one or more people bending, breaking or ignoring rules of a club or even the DNR itself should NEVER be an excuse to allow them to ruin a hunt or an entire season for the rest of us.

The last season turned out to produce the perfect opportunity to establish myself as the hunter portrayed throughout this book... through a strange series of events. Once again, I started the season with the mission of taking a trophy buck with my bow. Surely that accomplishment would display to all that I was truly an authority on learning to hunt. (Perhaps I should have taken the time to read the pages I had so earnestly written on the subject)! My hunting buddy Michael and I had scouted and found, tracked, photographed and patterned multiple bucks that would fit the bill nicely. VERY NICELY! (I pause to take the opportunity to point out how well QDMA tactics work. Having started on a raw piece of property with very small bucks and a grossly unproportioned buck to doe ratio, we, seven years later were managing a property with a well-balanced herd and for this area... some very nice bucks.) Back to the last lesson...

this time I had help. Michael knew what I was attempting and why. He unselfishly set, aside his goals to help me with mine very much in the Balenacre tradition of good hunting partners. He's become a good hunting partner and a great friend. On par with Vernon. We chose the two best bucks on this parcel and vowed that one would of us would take one of them and the other would get the other. Which didn't really matter, either would easily serve my purpose and, in Balenacre tradition, I would be more than happy to help my buddy drag the better of the two out of the woods. We strategized and put into motion several plans which evolved as the season progressed. Michael transitioned through the different seasons armed with whatever weapon was legal at that moment. I stubbornly held on to my bow. Many other animals came under our bead during that season but neither of us took the shot. We were patiently waiting for one of the two we had chosen. To say that I had become consumed would have been an understatement. Possessed, obsessed or even addicted would have been a more accurate description. My lovely wife had planned a wonderful vacation to Cabo San Lucas, and I was reluctant to go! The lure of hunting one and only one buck had engulfed my season. I somehow managed to realize that I was not enjoying myself... rather I was compelled. Eventually the need for meat overcame us both. Actually, even that is not completely the truth. Michael took a decent buck towards the end of the season. I took a doe, and my hunting buddy burned his second buck tag to provide meat for me so I could continue my quest. That unselfish act bested anything that all my Balenacre hunting buddies had ever done for me...not that they wouldn't have...

I continued my "quest for the grail". I had a very good friend whose company shared the same office building as mine. He and I had been talking for over a year about me taking him and his son on their first hunt. My very favorite thing about hunting. Two actually rolled into one and a father and son experience to boot. It was right in front of me and I was ignoring the opportunity. When I finally got around to taking them out they were both so excited. The days before we were to go I went out to the property to put out some acorns I had gathered to better their chances. When the day arrived, my buddy Bernie introduced me to his son Tom. A fine young man who was beside himself with anticipation of the experience that was unfolding before him. He was dressed for the hunt and stoked would have been an apt description of him. We loaded our gear into my truck and pilled in. On the drive out, we made small talk for a while then I engaged Tom about the hunt. Bernie is an avid researcher and had studied up on most of the things I was going over with his young son. I showed him my buck call and my doe can. Letting him practice and play with it for the entire drive. Somewhere in that drive a realization hit me that I was enjoying myself for the first time since the early season when Michael and I were scouting together. We finally arrived at the property. I took them over to our sign in board and showed Tom where we were and where we were going to be going to hunt. We explained the reason and the value of pinning in our positions. I let Tom do the job. We drove over to the gate of the parcel we'd be hunting. Tom looked on wide eyed as his father and I readied ourselves for the hunt. We began that magical "first walk" into the world that I had so deeply grown to love. I showed them how to walk silently. How to peer through the trees to what might lay beyond. How to pass into an opening ready for a shot opportunity. Movements that were now part of my DNA. But all of these, new and somewhat mystical to them. At that moment, I realized that the self-implied trophy quest to prove to my readers that I was an expert was exactly the opposite of everything I believed...Everything I'd grown to love about hunting...It had been there all along, right before my eyes on the very pages that I had written so diligently over the years. The teacher had become the student. It had taken only the wondrous eyes of a ten-year-old boy to open my eyes to the truth...

MORE THAN ANYTHING ELSE ABOUT HUNTING, I LOVE SHARING IT WITH OTHERS FOR THE FIRST TIME!

Learning to hunt has changed my life forever. Becoming part of this "lifestyle" has opened many new and exciting doors for me. Associating with those who know how to fend for themselves has changed my life forever. The confidence it has instilled in me and in my abilities to survive in the wilderness has made me an outdoorsman. Learning how and when to handle firearms has allowed me to become a better protector of myself, my family and others around me. There are far too many shows on TV about people who ended up in peril because they didn't heed the one lesson that has been repeated over and over again throughout this book..."

If you don't know something, ask someone who does"!

Some of the lessons I've learned were about handling people. Others were about respecting nature and loving the animals within it. Some helped in dealing with adversity, while others were about how to deal with life's successes. Many positive thoughts, actions and deeds have been introduced to me while I was learning to hunt. It can quite easily do the same for you and your children.

Come join us, one way or the other.
Please, be our guests while you're
LEARNING TO HUNT

CPSIA information can be obtained
at www.ICGtesting.com
Printed in the USA
BVHW051132050123
655630BV00008B/384